Focused Leadership

How to Improve Student Achievement

Richard T. Castallo

The Scarecrow Press, Inc.
A Scarecrow Education book published
with the American Association
of School Administrators
Lanham, Maryland, and London
2001

SCARECROW PRESS, INC.
A Scarecrow Education Book

Published in the United States of America
by Scarecrow Press, Inc.
4720 Boston Way
Lanham, Maryland 20706
www.scarecrowpress.com

4 Pleydell Gardens, Folkestone
Kent CT20 2DN, England

British Library Cataloguing-in-Publication Information Available

Library of Congress Cataloging-in-Publication Data

Castallo, Richard T., 1950–
   Focused leadership : how to improve student achievement / Richard Castallo.
     p. cm — (Scarecrow education book)
   Includes bibliographical references (p.).
   ISBN 0-8108-4063-4 (pbk. : alk. paper)
    1. School improvement programs—United States. 2. Educational leadership—United
States. 3. Academic achievement—United States. I. Title.

LB2822.82 .C376 2001
371.2'00973—dc21   2001049014

DEDICATION

Some five years ago, I was invited to participate in discussions with the members of the Glens Falls, New York school board and their superintendent, Tom McGowan, to discuss two important goals they wished to pursue. The first was to improve public relations. They felt they had an excellent small city school district that was often overlooked for various reasons by people who might be moving into the area. The second goal was to develop this public relations effort based on real results and not just "smoke and mirrors."

This initial discussion lead to a number of others, and ultimately, to the development of a plan and practices developed by the board and members of their fine administrative and teaching staff. Several of these practices are described in this text and many have been used in other school districts in different states. I thank this fine group of people; their interest and passion for children shows that there is indeed a role for everyone in the improvement of learning.

Contents

Foreword

The start of the twenty-first century finds a national spotlight shining on our public education system and its leaders, with greater intensity than most times in our history. This scrutiny creates heightened pressure for results; at the national, state and local levels policymakers and parents and business leaders all demand not only that schools be available to all students, but that schools prepare *all* students to learn and achieve to high standards.

The battles of the last decades of the twentieth century were over access to quality education for minorities, for those with disabilities, for recent immigrant students. Those battles are largely won; the next campaign is to demonstrate that the schools can serve their diverse populations well.

It has always been a challenge to navigate the rocky terrain of scarce resources, unfunded mandates, board politics, community opinion and education bureaucracies, but never more than today. Educational leaders must be knowledgeable about instruction, curriculum, finances, transportation, and student safety. The need to know how to collaborate with their board, to negotiate with staff, and to communicate effectively with diverse—and often divergent—community groups.

We have not lacked for proposed solutions to the task of educating our young people. Indeed, Richard Castallo suggests that we have suffered from too many scattered initiatives. He calls instead for a sustained focus for our efforts and says unequivocally that the focus should be student achievement.

Despite the promises and potential of strategic planning efforts, mission and goals alone will not result in improved student achievement because teachers, board members and parents are typically not sufficiently involved in the process. The result is a lack of understanding of the time and commitment required to create enduring change and an unfortunate tendency to try for a quick fix.

The principles of focused leadership—assessment, systems building, collaboration and communication—provide a solid structure for improvement. While Castallo does not minimize the hard work required to create a different culture in a school system, his approach is based on common sense and his own experience.

This book focuses on the role of the board, central administration, and building leadership in creating and maintaining the trust and continuous learning essential for student achievement. Using stories and concrete examples from several school districts, Castallo offers a multitude of suggestions for getting started on the important route to improved learning for all students. With persistence, school system leaders can move their districts toward systemic progress.

Paul D. Houston, Ph.D
Executive Director
American Association of School Administrators

CHAPTER 1

Are We Getting the Results We Want?

I have a few standard questions that I ask students in my educational administration classes: *How many of you have mission statements in your school or school district?* Virtually all of them raise their hands. Next, I ask: *How many of you have developed strategic plans in your school district?* About half typically respond affirmatively. I then ask: *Would anyone sitting here please describe curriculum changes or new teaching approaches that you are using as a result of your mission statement or strategic plan?*

I have asked these questions for several years and the answers have been consistent. Either no one, or at best only a couple of students, responded positively to the last question. In other words, the significant amounts of money put into generating mission statements and strategic plans have not typically translated into better instruction for children. Leithwood and Aitken (1995) note why strategic planning has failed to deliver on its intentions: "Unmanageably large numbers of 'priorities' are identified; so much turbulence is created in the organization's environment that well-targeted improvements become impossible to make; and initial increases in commitment to the organizations' directions are followed by pessimism and disillusionment as the school or district finds it impossible to follow through on much of its plan" (p. 3).[1] Christopher Bart, a business professor at McMaster University in Hamilton, Ontario, noted in a *New York Times* article that while some organizations have found value and direction in mission statements: "The overall conclusion is that, in any sample of mission statements, the vast majority are not worth the paper that they are written on and should not be taken with any degree of seriousness."[2]

One might go further and observe that since the classroom is "where the action is" and the teacher is the primary individual for delivering that action, strategic planning is doomed from the start if it is intended to improve student achievement. First, many strategic planning activities fail to provide widespread teacher involvement. While it is commendable to involve community members, administrators, board members, and others in the strategic planning process, they are not the ones working with children on a daily basis. Second, if improvement is to occur, organizational planning skills have little to do with the skills needed to plan and instruct in the classroom. Certainly, good planning is important for a school district or any organization.

The conclusions of our discussions usually end up something like this:

1. There is no program that will fix all of the deficiencies that exist in education. For that matter,
2. It is unlikely that any one program will permanently remedy even a single deficiency. And finally,
3. Many programs fail to fix even the single deficiency that they set out to conquer!

In attempting to deal with the most important issue in education today, improving student achievement, we have tried to find a magic wand rather than address the problems of academic performance in a systematic manner. Instead of trying to find cure-alls, board of education members, administrators, and teachers who serve the children in our schools need to definitively look at where they want to be, collaboratively seek answers, and carefully monitor progress.

This calls for doing business differently. It means that we need to redefine the role of board of education members in pursuing greater educational achievement for the children in their schools. It means that administrators need to exercise skills and knowledge, which will result in students learning more. And most important, it means that the teachers who deliver the curriculum every day can make a significant difference when they apply effective instructional approaches and assessments.

Those who have studied and written about means of improving what goes on in schools have collected a lot of information about the change process, teaching techniques, scheduling strategies, and various other processes that take place in schools. This information has provided a valuable source of data about organizational and classroom approaches that in fact can contribute to better education. There is no need to re-tread this ground. We know the stages that occur in effective change efforts. We know that when properly implemented, change is more likely to occur when the people delivering the program are meaningfully involved, not just the recipients of orders from their superiors. We know that children have a better chance of becoming proficient readers when they have a strong phonics base from which to draw. We know that block scheduling can reduce violence in schools and increase time on task in classrooms. We know a whole lot of information. What we don't always know is why, when we do all of these things in some schools, results still don't improve.

THE FRUSTRATIONS OF TEACHERS

Couple the responses of the teachers in my classes with another phenomenon that is common to American education—the magic fix! The 1990s brought the latest in a long line of these "answers-to-all-of-our-problems" to education. The most recent is the standards movement. An assumption has been made that a new set of expectations will result in students being smarter and more able. Although this is a bold and noble effort, experienced teachers can easily refer to a number of other equally noble and bold initiatives that have taken place over the years that held similar promise: whole language and new math were going to fix our concerns with students lacking basic skills. Looping and block scheduling would reduce loss time and result in a jump in the achievement of both elementary and secondary students. Veteran teachers could easily generate a list of many other initiatives that held great promise, including middle-level education, interdisciplinary teams, multiple intelligences, reduced class size, technology, use of brain research, reading in the content areas, and alternative education, to name just a few.

Such efforts are admirable. They have caused many educators to be excited about new possibilities. Often, those who have initiated these efforts have been able to point to improvements in student achievement and attitude. However, a number of other schools have implemented these same efforts and failed to get similar results. Although such efforts are usually put into effect with good intentions, none have ever shown a systematic, causal link between usage and improved student achievement.

The question, then, is fairly simple. Why haven't any of these initiatives delivered the dramatic improvements hoped for? So many were initiated with such great fanfare and promise, yet the results never panned out. As one teacher put it while discussing the standards effort—"Here we go again."

While administrators often become frustrated by teachers' lack of willingness to adopt new practices, we should examine why so many veteran educators become cynical when asked to undergo new forms of staff development, adopt new practices, or implement new curriculum. The following are common responses: "The central office adopts a new series but then fails to provide support for the materials or supplies we need." Another is "State Ed tells us our kids are going to be tested using new assessments but then fails to share sample assessments with us ahead of time or let us see the results afterward. Then our scores are published in the local paper and we look like we aren't doing anything!" Finally, the big one: "The new administrator is just trying to build up his resume and then he'll be gone to a bigger and better job."

Several factors contribute to the frustration of teachers. While those in leadership positions have heard these comments over the years, few schools have been able to remedy them in any kind of systematic way. As a result, teachers have learned the waiting game. Perhaps the most popular quote in education has become so popular for a reason: "This, too, will pass."

THE FRUSTRATIONS OF ADMINISTRATORS

When we take the time to look at the various initiatives that we have witnessed over the years, one omission is obvious. There has been little effort to "stick-to" initiatives. The bandwagon is alive and well in education. With it, little attention has been given to long-term commitment or accountability. Many administrators are not trained in staff development efforts themselves and often lack the understanding needed to ensure that initiatives are implemented and incorporated into the instructional repertoire of their staff members. As a result, their credibility with staff is minimized when they are unable to participate in intelligent conversations about new programs.

Most administrators can count the number of times that "expectations" have been placed on them by the district office to improve grades and to implement new programs. In the meantime, concerns with school violence are at an all-time high, complex social problems have found their way into our schoolhouses, and the support to inner-city schools is drastically deficient in relation to that of their suburban neighbors. For those faced with keeping peace in a building so that teachers can teach or attending workshops aimed at implementing new initiatives, the choice is relatively easy.

In the meantime, principals, especially secondary principals, are viewed by staff members as unlikely sources for support when it comes to providing assistance in particular content areas: "She's never taught science and she thinks she can come in and observe me and tell me how to teach?!" Caught between the expectations of the central office and the difficulty in establishing credibility with staff as someone knowledgeable about teaching and learning, mid-level school leaders often find themselves satisfying neither.

While all this goes on, the ability of administrators to set direction has been reduced as a result of shared decision making (SDM). Although many would concur that the idea makes sense, the amount of time required for meetings results in other priorities being sacrificed. In addition, many schools have never clearly understood the purpose for SDM. Practiced in its most egalitarian way, SDM teams have been allowed to identify priorities to be addressed and too often have spent their time talking about whether students should be allowed to wear hats in school and chew gum. As a result, administrators struggle to find a balance between their responsibilities for maintaining a safe building, meeting the requirements of contractual obligations, establishing their own identities as instructional leaders, and, foremost, advocating for the children in their charge.

THE FRUSTRATIONS OF SCHOOL BOARD MEMBERS

While we have failed to fully realize our ability to utilize the talents of teachers and administrators to better serve students, another important group that has the potential to greatly affect the lives of children has also been underutilized—local boards of education. The role of board members is a mystery to many. Most people are not quite sure of what they do or how far their responsibility stretches. One popular description of the role of the school board is "board members make policy and administrators implement it." While catchy, this definition fails to recognize the conflicts that often arise due to a lack of understanding related to role. For instance, it might seem reasonable that a superintendent and his or her subordinate administrators should make decisions involving the hiring of staff. However, board of education members are required to vote on the hiring of individuals in order to make their appointments official. Likewise, promotions and tenure of staff members also require board approval. Boards in most states are also required to approve curriculum and staff development programs. Many board members see these as important functions and individual members might feel a responsibility to know more about a candidate before voting or more about a program before giving it approval. As a result, it is not unusual to see members ask for copies of personnel files or programs, often to the consternation of some administrators.

Academics, while the primary role of the school, is the one area in which most board members have the least amount of involvement or understanding. Having facilitated hundreds of board of education workshops, I have found that board members consistently report that they do not have enough discussion related to student achievement. Many would like to contribute more but do not know how to go about doing so. Likewise, many superintendents have been heard to complain that board members are inappropriately involved in the operations of the school district.

CHANGING ROLES

If we truly wish to improve how our students achieve, it is important to look at the roles of the various people who have responsibility for their learning. I have worked with almost 200 school districts and held hundreds of retreats with board of education members and school administrators. Several commonalities have surfaced as I worked with these groups, which seem to extend across state lines. First, many board members are very comfortable talking about the purchase of school buses, how to handle the financing of roofing projects, and whether or not there is a need to change the football coach. In addition, most boards, when surveyed, state that they spend little time talking about students and instruction, yet they believe that they should spend more time on this topic. When asked how much time they spend talking with professionals in the district (teachers and administrators) about student achievement, the answer is usually none.

Likewise, I was initially surprised to find (but have become used to it over the years) that the responses of administrators are very similar to board of education members. When surveyed, they, too, share a concern that instruction is not a topic of conversation at administrative staff meetings. In addition, faculty meetings are not commonly used for such discussions and although time is sometimes dedicated to student achievement at department or grade level meetings, the discussions that do occur are usually focused on results rather than practices.

What, then, should be the role of various parties? What can board of education members do to actually benefit the learning that goes on in classrooms? How can board members interact with professional staff members without getting caught up in the daily operations of the schools and maintain their role as policymakers? Furthermore, what should be the relationship of administrators to board members, to their superintendent and central office counterparts, as well as to the staff members in their schools? And finally, how do teachers, those who are the most important professionals in the schools when it comes to responsibility for student learning, know what is expected of them in terms of student achievement?

FOCUSED LEADERSHIP

Traditional efforts for raising student achievement may best be described as "shotgun approaches" to improvement. Whether we talk about strategic planning, standards-based education, new math/old math, phonics-based or whole language, critics continue to point to the poor educational showing of many of our schools as a basis of failure by educators.

If there is one commonality to this failure to progress, it may well have to do with the lack of specificity we look for in our results. Evidence of this is easy to find. Go to almost any school district and take a look at some common practices that we witness on a regular basis. Curriculum development money is often allocated based on requests by staff members who believe there is a need to spend a week or two in the summer strengthening a particular content area. Several pieces are typically missing: requests are often the result of one staff member who never communicated with other departmental or grade-level colleagues before asking for support. The individual staff member often ends up working alone on her effort, with no system in place to ensure that colleagues receive the material along with an explanation of how it should be used once it has been completed. The materials often are not related to standards, benchmarks, assessments, or any other curricular documents.

Staff development practices are often similar. A motivational speaker spends two hours making staff members feel good. Unfortunately, a few days later they might not be feeling so good about their students' results on a unit test. Or superintendent conference days are planned around the latest and greatest new hot topic in education, one that someone has decided that every teacher, K–12, regardless of content area, should hear. And one that ultimately has little or no impact on the performance of students in the science lab or geography classroom.

Such ineffectiveness exists within the daily systems that operate in schools as well. Evaluation systems are considered a sham by many veteran teachers. Often administrators have little credibility with staff members, who do not believe that someone can legitimately observe them when the person doing the observing might have little understanding of the content area being taught or perhaps was not seen as a master teacher before joining the ranks of administration.

New teachers are often hired and tenured based almost entirely on the interpersonal impressions they make, rather than on their knowledge of content and ability to deliver that content to students. Likewise, the lack of effective orientation programs on the part of school districts often leads many bright young people to leave teaching within their first few years to look for employment in other areas.

The movement throughout the nation to improve student achievement has provided a focus for the ends we should have in mind. However, the shotgun approach we have practiced over the years has provided no consistent measurable results. Furthermore, the sometimes frenetic rush from one new program to another leaves us looking foolish in the eyes of parents and other observers, as empty promises become disappointing realities.

The adoption of *Focused Leadership* does not require changing or adopting a new program. It does not recommend that more money needs to be spent on staff or curriculum development. What it does require is a look at present practices within a school system, as well as effective practices that may be used in the schools. It requires a common-sense approach to educating students that is systematic and based on specific needs. It is also based on the understanding that "effective change takes time" but that we have overused that adage, and every child who goes through our schools as they now operate may be getting cheated if we do not focus our energies with greater urgency. *Focused Leadership* requires a different way of looking at the roles and responsibilities of the major actors in a school system—board of education members, administrators, and teachers. It requires that "blame" be replaced by collaboration and that when students succeed, all succeed; likewise, when students fail, all have failed—and we then need to figure out why and do something about it.

The districts that have adopted this approach have improved their students' scores. These improvements have not been the result of miracles. In each of them, board members have taken a serious and involved interest in what is happening in classrooms. Administrators have gained skills and knowledge that have allowed them to shift their attention from supervision for monitoring to supervision for leadership. Teachers and administrators now discuss student outcomes and expectations on a regular basis, with an eye toward planning for improving student results.

The purpose of this book is to suggest practical approaches that have been used in school districts that have had success in raising student achievement. No district uses all of the strategies described. Likewise, where a strategy is implemented in various districts, it often looks different. Adaptations have taken place based on organizational history—the politics of the particular school and districts and individual needs of users and students. Each district is unique, and the idea of a "cookie-cutter" approach, in which the same program or initiative can be replicated without significant adaptation, is illogical. It is imperative that each district be looked at individually and approaches planned accordingly.

This book will provide a number of common areas that need to be addressed and also suggests ways to provide the flexibility in deciding what is being offered, when it will be offered, and how it will be offered. Although it is important that certain tasks be accomplished—for instance, data-based goal setting—the process for doing this not only *might* vary but *should* vary from one district to another.

It only makes sense that adjustments must occur from district to district in the way we go about implementing any kind of a change effort. The political climate, resources available, labor relations, past successes and failures, and competency of staff are just a few factors that require serious consideration when we decide how to go about taking on a new initiative. Because of this, careful planning by leaders is crucial to the acceptance and ultimate institutionalizing of any effort aimed at improvement.

PRINCIPLES OF *FOCUSED LEADERSHIP*

Although the approaches may vary, some important principles must be in place in order to effectively improve student achievement. These include the following:

1. Honest assessment of student performance—Do we objectively analyze and determine how well students are performing? Do we use what we learn to inform instruction?
2. Systems building—Do we regularly look at ways to improve practices that are focused on raising student achievement? Are our everyday practices, such as teacher evaluation, instructional planning, and evaluation, focused on student outcomes?
3. Ongoing collaboration—Have we developed a belief system that "we're all in this together" and success, as well as failure to progress, is the responsibility of all parties? Is the climate in the schools "nonthreatening"? Do the building and district shared decision-making groups truly work toward better results?
4. Regular communication—Do we have structures in place to ensure that successes are shared? Do staff members know how, as well as have the time, to reflect on what they do and share insights with their peers?

These principles provide an underpinning for improvement. They mandate, by their nature, accountability of users. After all, if one honestly *assesses* how well students perform, then one is better equipped to acknowledge the circumstances in which students have learned. If realistic comparisons are being made and results are not as good as they should be, then we need to determine what *systems* we (teachers, administrators, board members, and parents) should be reviewing for consideration. The best way to review systems is through *collaboration,* since multiple views are likely to be richer and more informative than those of one individual. Finally, once conclusions are made, they need to be *communicated* to others who can also benefit from the implementation of new knowledge.

The following pyramid outlines leadership roles for board of education members, district administrators, and building staff as we move toward maximizing student achievement. Listing these three roles is not intended to suggest that they are the only important parties to children's learning. Parents as well as children themselves have important parts to play. The purpose of this book is to focus on developing a climate and structures that school people can readily adopt. Since our behavior and attitudes are in our immediate control, the emphasis here is to address those areas that school people can change relatively easily and on short notice. The remainder of this book provides descriptions of the roles of board of education members, administrators, and teachers and how the roles of each of these groups might be reexamined and performed in a school district. Specific examples that might be adopted are also provided.

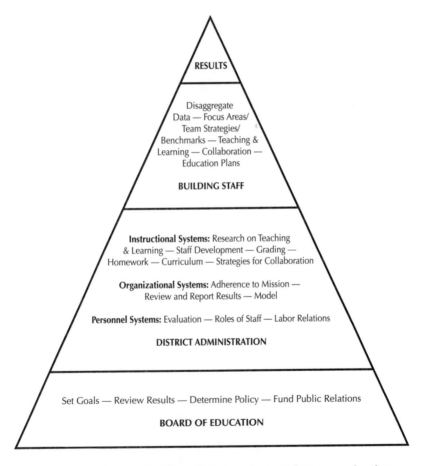

RESULTS

Disaggregate
Data — Focus Areas/
Team Strategies/
Benchmarks — Teaching &
Learning — Collaboration —
Education Plans

BUILDING STAFF

Instructional Systems: Research on Teaching
& Learning — Staff Development — Grading —
Homework — Curriculum — Strategies for Collaboration

Organizational Systems: Adherence to Mission —
Review and Report Results — Model

Personnel Systems: Evaluation — Roles of Staff — Labor Relations

DISTRICT ADMINISTRATION

Set Goals — Review Results — Determine Policy — Fund Public Relations

BOARD OF EDUCATION

Assessment System Building Collaboration and Communication

Although a number of "hands-on" materials are shared, it must be understood that the materials and strategies do *not* stand alone. Even though they might be practical and provide an efficient way for school leaders to get started, what is equally important are the foundation principles of *assessment, system building, collaboration,* and *communication.* If these are not embedded in practice, it is likely that efforts to improve student achievement will indeed become "just another innovation."

NOTES

1. Leithwood, Kenneth A. and Aitken, Robert. *Making Schools Smarter: A System Monitoring School and District Progress.* Thousand Oaks, Calif.: Corwin Press (1995).

2. Greenhouse, Steven. "Mission Statements—Words That Can't Be Set to Music," *New York Times,* February 13, 2000.

CHAPTER 2

The Role of the Board of Education

Having had the opportunity to work with a number of school board members, I cannot recall ever meeting one who did not want students to provide evidence of high academic achievement. This is not to say that a few members did not have other matters that they felt had more importance to them, such as fielding a winning sports team or seeing that a Talented and Gifted Program (which, of course, their daughter or son would enroll in) was started. However, most board members I have met are hard-working, sincere people who really want the best for all children and believe that improving student results is very important. Although most board members share this common interest, neither they nor many superintendents are quite sure of the role of school board members in this process. For that matter, some are not even sure if they should play a role at all.

Board members can provide significant support for learning in five areas. These include goal setting, reviewing results, determining policy, providing funding, and orchestrating positive public relations, both within and outside of the schools. This is where the democratic process of school leadership can be seen working at its best. Boards were originally constructed to provide local oversight to the functioning of schools. While the responsibility given to them was broad, little specific guidance on how to operate was ever provided in legislation. As a result, we have seen school boards in which members take a very active role in both the policy making and administration of their school districts, as well as boards that attempt to strictly observe and respect the "policy versus administration" dichotomy.

When it comes to their role in instructional leadership, boards need direction from their superintendents. Together, they need to decide on how to best identify challenging goals that will be viewed as realistic by the teachers and administrators who are in the schools. *There is no one correct way to do this.* As noted previously, too often we look for prescriptions in education that will provide the magic answer. There isn't one. Changes in board members, superintendents, building administrators, and teacher leadership all have something to do with the best way to implement a change effort in a school. Many other factors also come into play—historical events that have shaped the relationships between various parties, parental expectations, and labor relations climates, to name just a few. As a result, while the board's role is extremely important in taking the lead in providing expectations, it is really the superintendents' job to guide school boards in working with school constituents and building agendas for discussion.

THREE APPROACHES TO INVOLVING THE BOARD IN SETTING GOALS

In an effort to begin conversations on improving student achievement, the superintendent is responsible for setting the stage through discussions with board members about their role and interest in moving student achievement to greater levels. The superintendent should emphasize the board's role in direction setting (not implementation). Using a board of education self-evaluation instrument in conjunction with a board retreat is an excellent way to start this discussion, as well as of beginning to clarify members' roles. An evening or two or a Saturday dedicated to this one topic allows for focus in a relaxed, open atmosphere. In addition, follow-up meetings might be scheduled to educate board members on how to review and interpret information. Time should also be provided to deal with queries that board members might have on any specific concerns before they meet to discuss recommendations with the administrative team.

In working with boards of education in setting academic goals, we have observed three different approaches, each with success:

Option 1: Board → Administrator → Staff

The first approach involves discussing student achievement data with the board and superintendent. Board members review student results in relation to neighboring districts, to past performance within the district, and from year-to-year and building-to-building data. As the instructional leader of the school district, the superintendent needs to be well versed in what the data mean and whether legitimate extenuating circumstances make certain results look significantly positive or negative. It is not the superintendent's job to dictate to the board but rather to interpret and recommend as appropriate. Most board members have not gone through schools of education, nor do they have expertise in data analysis. Superintendents, along with other internal staff or an outside consultant, should have these experiences and skills in their backgrounds and be able to provide some education for board members.

- Following this, the superintendent meets with central office and building administrators to review the board's discussion and ask for the administrators' opinions and reactions. Some common achievement goals should be reached, and if disagreement does exist, administrators should be prepared to explain why and make other recommendations to take back to the board.
- A joint meeting of the board and administrators should take place to tentatively adopt the district's goals.
- Once tentative goals are reached, they should be shared at the building level by the superintendent or principals. Staff members need to know that the role of the board is to set the direction for the district, and they have done this by carefully reviewing and discussing information. The same information that the board reviewed should be given to the staff. Data from within, as well as data that provides a comparison to similar districts, other states, and national sources should be provided. If appropriate, international (world-class schools') data may be useful. Staff members should have the opportunity to comment on the goals. This is *not* intended to be an opportunity to disagree with the board's right to set goals. That is not an option. It is a chance to add or make suggestions for revisions to the goals being presented.
- Any comments should be shared with the board by the superintendent and then a final set of goals adopted.
- Once adopted, goals should be shared with the community. This can be done through newsletters, public forums, a district portfolio, or a district education plan. These latter outlets should also include a brief description of activities and timelines that will be used by the district to pursue its goals and that are discussed later in this book.

Option 2: Administrators → Board

- The second approach involves administrators providing direction to the board prior to its adoption of goals.
- Administrators then review the data from the variety of sources described previously and come up with recommendations to the board. The rationale for these recommendations should be provided in discussions with the board. Charts, graphs, and tables are all useful tools. Administrators should also try to provide a range of possible goals rather than recommendations that appear to be absolutes. Board members provide a unique perspective that should be respected. For instance, one board, after listening to the administrators, asked why there was no "character education" goal. The board had made a significant commitment to character education, and some members felt that evidence of its effectiveness should be available to justify the costs. A member on another board suggested that goals involving student achievement should consider student participation in extracurriculars because the board had been provided with research that suggested that students who participated in clubs and sports tended to do better academically.
- Once the board adopts tentative goals, these should be communicated by the superintendent and board president to the staff and community.

Option 3: Staff and Administrators → Board

Some districts prefer to have administrators and staff talk about student achievement goals and then take recommendations to the board of education. This is certainly a valid option, but some important preplanning should take place. First, it is extremely important for the superintendent (and project consultant, if one is involved) to meet with administrators to discuss results and provide them with an overview of what potential goals might look like. This will ensure more consistency, especially when there are multiple buildings at certain grade levels. Second, it is also important that people are speaking the "same language." Developing targets is a form of accountability that is foreign to most school people, and the concept of specificity in developing targets must be clearly understood. Finally, it needs to be emphasized that the board itself will ultimately adopt goals, and this needs to be communicated to staff members so there is no misunderstanding.

- This approach asks teachers to review the same data described previously. This can be done at the school level by the building principal or in a committee made up of staff members. If the latter, the tentative goals that result should still be taken back to the staff members in the buildings for their comments. Whichever format is used, it is crucial to emphasize that goals must be *student achievement*-related. This is a difficult concept for many educators. At the same time, teachers need to be assured that whether or not goals are reached will not be the responsibility of just one classroom teacher. Administrators will be called upon to provide ideas, strategies, support for training, equipment, and materials. Board members will also be involved by providing their support. If, for example, a high-stakes test is given to students at the end of the third grade, teachers in kindergarten, first, and second grades have to work together in a team effort. The new joke in education—*no one wants to be a third (or fourth or fifth) grade teacher*—is rooted in the fact that many of these educators feel that they are being congratulated or criticized simply because they are the teacher in the particular year a test is given.
- Once goals have been identified by teachers and administrators, these are shared with the board of education for review, final adoption, and publication to the community.

As noted, each of these approaches has been used with good success. The history and climate in the district have much to do with our deciding which one (or even a further adaptation) would best work in a particular setting. What is most important is grounding the approach to be used in the three concepts stressed at the bottom of the *Improving Student Achievement Pyramid*—in other words, *Assessment* that is objective, regular, and focused on student results; *Systems Building* aimed at improving achievement based on student data; and *Communication and Collaboration,* which sends the message that all parties are working on this as a team and then sharing the efforts and outcomes with all stakeholders.

PREPARING TO SET GOALS

The role of the board is to look at the "big picture" and set direction for the district through the goal-setting process. The details related to disaggregating data and then prescribing instructional practices should be left to administrators and teachers. Goals should be developed at all organizational levels of a school district, and benchmarks for comparison should come from a variety of sources. Examples of goals generated through the processes described previously are then formally accepted by boards of education. The following chart shows several examples of both elementary and secondary goals adopted by boards of education. Following the chart is a description of several goals.

District Wide Goals

THE _____ BOARD OF EDUCATION MAKES THE FOLLOWING COMMITMENTS:

1. STUDENT ACHIEVEMENT ON ALL STATE ASSESSMENTS WILL BE GREATER THAN SIMILAR AND ALL PUBLIC SCHOOLS IN THE STATE.
2. STUDENT ACHIEVEMENT ON ALL STATE ASSESSMENTS WILL BE GREATER THAN THE AVERAGE SCORES OF STUDENTS FROM THE PREVIOUS THREE YEARS.
3. STUDENT ACHIEVEMENT ON THE ABC TEST WILL RESULT IN ____% OF STUDENTS GAINING AT LEAST ONE YEAR'S GROWTH IN READING AND MATH.
4. BY 2000–2001, ____% OF STUDENTS WILL SCORE AT OR ABOVE LEVEL 3 ON STATE TESTS AT THE 4TH AND 8TH GRADE LEVELS AND ____% OR BETTER ON STATE EXAMS.
5. BY 2002–03, THE HIGH SCHOOL WILL RANK IN THE TOP 150 HIGH SCHOOLS OF THE STATE ON STATE TEST PERFORMANCE.
6. THERE WILL BE A ____% DECREASE IN DISCIPLINE REFERRALS, AND ____% OF STAFF MEMBERS WILL REPORT THAT IMPROVEMENT OCCURRED IN CORE VALUES (E.G., RESPECT, HONESTY, DIGNITY).

(continued)

Different levels of attainment are used for various goals to ensure that each one is fair and relevant. Although the goals are important, they must be flexible. It might turn out, after we implement efforts to meet goals, that some are not practical. For instance, if a test that has been used to measure progress in the past is dropped and a new one adopted, or if the results on a state test are dismal across most of the school districts in the state, it may not be a fair barometer by which to judge outcomes in a given year. Wherever possible, multiple means of looking at results should take place. The following provide examples:

7. SECONDARY	INCREASE PERCENTAGE OF (continued)	
% PASSING	TEST	% WITH DISTINCTION
10%	ENGLISH—GRADE 11	10%
60%	MATH A	10%
AT 82%—MAINTAIN	GLOBAL STUDIES	RTS
RTS (REMAIN THE SAME)	FOREIGN LANGUAGE	Increase 3 yr. avg. by 5%
Increase 3 yr. avg. by 5%	AMERICAN HISTORY	Increase 3 yr. avg. by 5%
Increase 3 yr. avg. by 5%	EARTH SCIENCE	Increase 3 yr. avg. by 5%
Increase 3 yr. avg. by 5%	BIOLOGY	Increase 3 yr. avg. by 5%
70% PASSING	PHYSICS	INCREASE 5%
Increase 3 yr. avg. by 5%	MATH I	Increase 3 yr. avg. by 5%
Increase 3 yr. avg. by 5%	MATH II	Increase 3 yr. avg. by 5%
Increase 3 yr. avg. by 5%	MATH III	Increase 3 yr. avg. by 5%
RTS	ACCELERATED MATH	Increase 3 yr. avg. by 5%

1. *Student achievement on all state assessments will be greater than similar and all public schools in the state.*
   Note that "similar" and "all public schools" are used as a basis for comparison. At this time, more than thirty-six states publicly report school data,[1] making access to such information relatively easy. In addition, "all public schools" includes every reporting district in the state. Critics may find such comparisons to be unfair and might point to certain demographic factors that cause skewed results. For instance, in states with extremely large cities such as New York or Los Angeles, statewide test results could be significantly impacted because as many as a third of the students in the state attend the schools in that city's one large district. For many people, statistics are often confusing and seem easy to manipulate. Even when statistics are explained in a clear and fair manner, some people will never be convinced. This makes it important that we use other sources for comparison. "Similar" schools are those that are categorized as similar by makeup—for instance, urban, suburban, or rural.
2. *Student achievement on all state assessments will be greater than the average scores of students from the previous three years.*
   In this example, districts are only compared to themselves, not to others. Average scores for the last three years are determined and graphed. Stakeholders then must examine the data and initiate a goal-setting process in which they analyze strengths and weaknesses

in student performance, research their options, and implement efforts that will improve performance.

3. *Student achievement on the ABC Test will result in 90 percent of students gaining at least one year's growth in reading and math.*
Using a norm-referenced test, we can track results against what should be statistically accepted as normal growth. Where students are not meeting expectations, we will once again go through the problem-solving process.

4. *By 2002–03, the high school will rank in the top 150 high schools in the state on state test performance.*
With the large number of states now publicly reporting data, individual districts are faced with a district report card that is similar to those students have received over the years. Although student report cards are private, the district report card is public in most states. Assuming that what is being taught and tested is sound and relates to the written curriculum, it is crucial that curriculum, instruction, and leadership are all aligned in order to maximize the results, which will be shared with the community.

5. *There will be a 25 percent decrease in discipline referrals, and 90 percent of staff members will report that improvement occurred in core values (e.g., respect, honesty, and dignity).*
Much of the information generated through the Effective Schools literature and other related research tells us that a safe and pleasant academic environment is imperative for student learning to take place. I have had staff members challenge the idea that you cannot evaluate some areas, such as behavior. On the contrary, virtually anything can be evaluated, and certainly the results of programs such as character education are a good example. Educators need to ask themselves the question: Why did we do this? Once they answer that question, they need to determine the kind of data that would tell them whether they are moving in the right direction. Thus, data related to students' behavior toward fellow students and staff could be collected. The number of bus and cafeteria referrals might be reported. Anecdotes, observations, and surveys of attitudes of students, teachers, support staff, and parents would also provide a view of whether an initiative has had a positive effect.

Even though the preceding examples are listed as elementary goals, they need not be restricted to the early grades. Many could be used at the secondary level as well. Goals at the elementary level should be fairly narrow and focused. We have a tendency to want to solve all of our problems at one time and, while noble, this can be so overwhelming that our efforts become fragmented. No more than two areas should be targeted in a given year. We are finding that language arts is probably the most common area of interest in most schools. Thus, goals aimed at improving English and language arts abilities might be one priority area. Likewise, in many schools, math is seen as a major concern. Some districts decide to emphasize social studies or science. Exactly which area to focus on should be driven by student performance. If a review of data over the last three to five years shows that students are scoring well in math, it is probably best to focus on a different content area. If the state has come out with a new science assessment, and science has not been an area of strength, then it would make sense to focus on science.

Since secondary schools are organized differently from elementary, and we want to have virtually all staff members working toward the improvement of student achievement, at least one goal should be generated in each secondary content area. The examples provided in the following chart were developed by combinations of teachers, administrators, and board members and ultimately adopted by boards:

Secondary Students' Achievement Goals: Increase . . .		
% Passing State Exam	Test	% Scoring at Distinction
10%	English—Grade 11	10%
60%	Math A	10%
at 82%—maintain	Global Studies	RTS
RTS (remain the same)	Foreign Language	Increase 3 yr. avg. by 5%/yr.
Increase 3 yr. avg. by 5%	American History	Increase 3 yr. avg. by 5%/yr.
Increase 3 yr. avg. by 5%	Earth Science	Increase 3 yr. avg. by 5%/yr.
Increase 3 yr. avg. by 5%	Biology	Increase 3 yr. avg. by 5%/yr.
70% passing	Physics	Increase 5%
Increase 3 yr. avg. by 5%	Math I	Increase 3 yr. avg. by 5%/yr
Increase 3 yr. avg. by 5%	Math II	Increase 3 yr. avg. by 5%/yr.
Increase 3 yr. avg. by 5%	Math III	Increase 3 yr. avg. by 5%/yr.
RTS	Accelerated Math	Increase 3 yr. avg. by 5%/yr.

This chart breaks down major content areas into two categories. The left column describes the goal for the percentage of students passing the state examination. The right column indicates the expected increase in the number of students functioning at the distinction level on the tests.

This district was moving toward counting all students, including special education, in its results during the subsequent school year. Consequently, the district determined that for certain students to "Remain the Same" (RTS) with their present scores would be significant since this group historically performed poorer than the general population. In some cases, there are teachers whose results are so strong that outperforming the previous year is almost impossible. For instance, the teacher who annually has 95 percent of all of his or her students pass the state exam has a much smaller margin for improvement than the teacher who had only 70 percent pass the test the previous year. In such cases, goals may involve trying to increase the percentage of students scoring at a "distinction level" or those receiving higher academic honors.

Although this chart outlines five content areas—English, science, math, social studies, and foreign language—teachers in special areas should not be ignored. Goals for teachers in "special areas" such as physical education, music, and art have included such things as participation in competitions (art and music), attitudes toward lifelong participation (physical education and music), and involvement in elective courses (art, music, home economics). Essentially, staff members in these areas need to ask themselves what they want students to know, be able to do, or believe as a result of experiences in their programs. Once they answer these questions, corresponding goals can be developed. In the examples given here, students may be evaluated differently—for instance, through surveys or participation rather than by a standardized test.

RECOGNIZING POSITIVE RESULTS

The steps for goal setting described thus far relate to the first year of the process. Organizing, setting goals, implementing efforts, and monitoring their progress are essential parts of any attempt to initiate improvement. However, it is important not to become complacent. Once the process has begun, it is necessary to maintain the energy and enthusiasm needed to continue. Doing this is a major responsibility of the board of education.

In one district, for instance, the board reviewed results from the first year, acknowledged the positive outcomes that occurred, and developed a number of activities for providing recognition. Some of these included:

- The board president and superintendent walking through the schools and stopping to talk with staff members about their positive results;
- The board president and vice president being present on the first day of school and greeting staff members as they walk in;
- The board president calling new staff members to welcome them to the district and emphasizing the importance of the contribution they will be making;
- The board having centerpieces and desserts in faculty rooms on the first day of school, as well on as Teacher Appreciation Day;
- The board providing awards to teachers and volunteers for service;
- The board publishing a newsletter to the community, announcing goals, and praising results; and
- The board's Curriculum Subcommittee meeting with grade levels and content areas to hear about efforts they are making and to provide support wherever possible.

THE BOARD OF EDUCATION AND GOAL SETTING— SUBSEQUENT YEARS

Although pleased with the positive results, the same board recognized some areas that still fell below expectations. In addition to the continuing goals that had been established during Year 1, the board believed that two additional goals should be established. As a result of their discussion, board members came up with the following statement and asked administrators to develop it further:

1. *Science—By July 31, administrators should provide the board with a recommendation for a goal with measurable, student achievement–based criteria that can be used to monitor science results.*

   When presenting the goal, the board requested that the administrators give their views on the following questions, along with any other pertinent information the administrators felt should be shared.

   Discussion questions:
   ✓ Is curriculum appropriately aligned, K–12?
   ✓ Is there a need for staff development with instructional approaches?

✓ How are the interpersonal relationships between staff members and kids?

✓ Should the science department meet with the BOE Curriculum Committee to share its efforts and plans?

✓ Would outside consultant help be useful?

✓ Is an item analysis completed on major tests and acted upon?

✓ Are student efforts being communicated to parents?

✓ Is technology being effectively utilized?

2. *By August 31, develop a plan and measurable goal(s) for improving communication between staff and students and staff and parents.*

Discussion questions:

✓ Are students given back tests and homework in a timely manner so that they can learn from their mistakes?

✓ Are grades and comments made on all Five Week Reports?

✓ Are sufficient grades available each marking period?

Even though Goal #2 is broader and focuses on communication, note that the end result is expected to be improved student achievement. This provides an excellent example of how student achievement has become the board's conscious focus when determining changes.

In another district the board of education was satisfied that the multiyear goals it had established during the first year only needed minor adjustments and instead focused on activities that would further its efforts toward success. As a result, the following management activities were developed:

1. *Invite administrators to meet with the BOE to report on progress in their buildings.*
   The board and superintendent decided to regularly schedule administrative updates to the board of education at specially scheduled meetings to focus on student achievement. In addition to keeping the board appraised of progress, this is also a good way to let the public see that student outcomes are a board priority.

2. *Continuation of staff development.*
   The board began a process of aligning money provided for staff development activities with specific student achievement goals.

The board was looking for direction from central administration on how to continue this process during Year 2.

3. *Development of a feedback system that would help various groups improve their performance.*

   The board believed that candid feedback is a crucial means for improvement—for board members themselves, as well as for administrators and teachers. In order to maximize this opportunity, the board agreed to self-evaluate annually, as well as to ask for an evaluation of its performance by the administrators who worked with it on a regular basis. In addition, the board asked that the superintendent conduct a feedback process that would allow administrators to share their perceptions of the superintendent's abilities as an instructional leader (a copy of the form *Superintendent Feedback by Administrative Staff* can be found in chapter 3). Likewise principals were asked to consider a similar form be completed on them by their instructional staff (see chapter 4). The ultimate goal would be to have instructional staff members conduct the same kind of survey with the students they serve.

4. *Develop a survey to be given to students and parents.*

   The board was interested in the perceptions of students and parents regarding school climate, expectations, students' views toward the school and their classroom, and other related topics. Categories of questions were related to factors associated with student performance.

5. *Improving school → parent relations.*

   Several board members reported personal experiences and comments from constituents regarding actions that would encourage greater parent-school collaboration. Administrators were asked to outline a plan to improve communication and relations between parents and the schools. Board members asked that the following be included as points for consideration:

   ✓ Teaching teachers how to conference with parents;

   ✓ Moving up parent conferences from the first eight weeks of school to the first four weeks;

   ✓ Providing an appropriate handout (outline) for parents at Open Houses;

   ✓ Developing a survey that parents could fill out before leaving an Open House; and

   ✓ Making sure that buildings are clean and attractive when events are being held at school.

6. *Celebrating the positive.*
   Board members believed that it was important to reinforce positive behaviors in order to better ensure their being repeated. A board committee was asked to come up with a plan for recognizing and rewarding staff members whenever possible.

What these boards of education did in these two cases is not a lot different from what is done by many teachers as they look at the progress of children in their classrooms. By setting goals and looking at the performance of an entire class, a teacher gains a good idea of the abilities of individuals and what can be done to motivate them. Likewise, a teacher also identifies those individual students with the greatest needs and earmarks extra resources to provide them with appropriate support.

The purpose and rationale for goal setting are simple. We cannot judge performance without knowing the criteria for success. This does not mean only the teachers in classrooms who are charged with the everyday delivery of content. It also includes administrators who oversee programs and instruction, boards that are responsible for seeing that support is provided for delivery, and parents who are responsible for follow through at home. Goals provide an objective comparison against which performance can be judged. Without them, we have no honest way to determine whether the children we serve are any better or worse off as a result of our efforts.

THE BOARD OF EDUCATION AND REVIEWING RESULTS

At the start of this book I talked about the often-humorous results of what I have come to call the Great Mission Statement Debacle. The millions of dollars spent on rhetoric that has had no real effect on student achievement are extremely discouraging. So how do we ensure that efforts to improve student achievement do not end up as the next decade's example of yet another educational initiative gone wrong?

Although the role of the board in goal setting is crucial to highlighting the importance of this commitment in a school, the process should not end with a list of lofty goals posted on office and classroom walls. Action is key to success. The penchant of educators to jump on the hottest bandwagons has done little to enhance education's reputation. Once a district commits to improved achievement, it is imperative that efforts continuously be identified to move in that direction. The board of education needs to be a leader in this effort.

As noted previously, a standard phrase in education is that the role of school boards is to develop policy, the role of administrators is to implement it. A nice adage, but one that we know contains a large gray area in which board members and superintendents often struggle over decision-making authority. Does taking a role in improving student achievement make for potential role conflict? Yes. It can be problematic, and boards and superintendents need to talk very openly about this before getting too far into such initiatives. Superintendents need to understand the pressure on board members. With public report cards now being generated, many board members hear from their constituents that the schools need to do more. For some board of education members, just the fact that people speak critically about the school is very difficult for them to handle. In addition, the hint of dissatisfaction may cause some board members to fear they will not be reelected. Finally, some believe that the outcomes that are being realized are not commensurate with the financial support that is provided and the schools need to do better. Regardless of the reason, once the commitment to improve has been made, board members need to become an ongoing part of the solution.

Goal setting is the crucial first step. Following this, board members must be involved in follow-up activities that let staff and community members know that the board is committed and moving forward. Perhaps the best way to describe the role of the board is to talk about what its role is, as well as what its role is not:

What *Should* Board Members Do to Play a Continuing Role in Improving Student Achievement?

- Curriculum subcommittees—many boards have a curriculum subcommittee that reviews requests for changes in the present program and makes recommendations to the full board. This subcommittee might instead meet monthly with a different content area or with various grade-level representatives to hear presentations on efforts related to goals. Such subcommittees should understand that they do *not* operate to make commitments or to critique. Their role is to listen and ask questions. The superintendent or his administrative designee should also participate as an ex-officio member of the curriculum subcommittee.
- The most effective school districts that we have had the opportu-

nity to work with actually have had mission statements that are operational. A board can set a tone by adopting a brief, focused mission statement that conveys its intentions and then use the statement as a basis for decision making. Johnson City, New York, for instance, developed the following: "All children will learn." These four words provide a reference for the board and staff. Note that this differs from the popular "all children *can* learn," which is often used in educational discussions. A subtle but extremely powerful difference, and later revisions to the statement maintained the same theme. Most important, board members should be conscious of the mission statement and be sure that their decisions are consistent with it.

- An important role for board members is to convey a climate of collaboration. Staff members should know that they have the support needed to move children toward greater academic success. Likewise, if success is not met at the intended levels, board members should send the message that staff members are not going to be isolated or blamed and that "We're in this together."
- Boards should annually evaluate their own effectiveness in relation to their commitment to improving student achievement. Many boards I work with conduct an annual retreat in which they review two areas, their own working relationships (board–board and board–superintendent) and the establishment of district goals. Some of these goals may be management-oriented and some should be educational.
- Once the board adopts goals, those of administrators, teachers, building teams, and others involved in the goal-setting process should complement those of the board. The Planning Cycle that follows illustrates how this process might be implemented to ensure continuity.

PLANNING CYCLE

At the top, or 12:00 o'clock point, the Board of Education conducts an annual self-evaluation. This is typically done in a retreat setting where members have the chance to discuss issues related to working relationships, as well as goals. Although many boards do this in the summer, this is not a requirement. Some may conduct their self-evaluations in the fall, shortly after school begins, and some in the spring as the

Planning Cycle

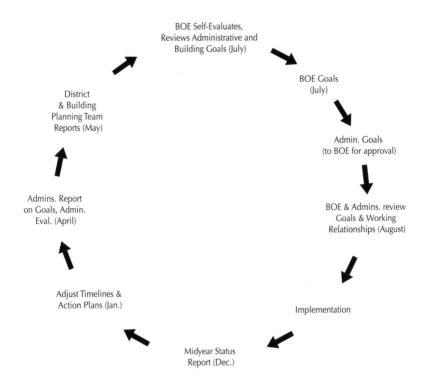

BOE Self-Evaluates,
Reviews Administrative and
Building Goals (July)

BOE Goals
(July)

District
& Building
Planning Team
Reports (May)

Admin. Goals
(to BOE for approval)

Admins. Report
on Goals, Admin.
Eval. (April)

BOE & Admins. review
Goals & Working
Relationships (August)

Adjust Timelines &
Action Plans (Jan.)

Implementation

Midyear Status
Report (Dec.)

school year is winding down. Prior to discussing their goals for the next
school year(s), board members should review goal efforts from the previous year by administrators and other stakeholder groups that are involved in these efforts in the district. Once that review is completed, the
goals that the board sets are used as a frame of reference for administrators in their own goal setting. The board's goals are shared by the superintendent (who is present at both sessions), since she will understand how the goals came to be determined, as well as the kinds of
discussions that took place. While the superintendent may have some
specific matters that she wants particular administrators to work on,
most administrative goals should complement those of the board.

Once administrators have met and set goals, some districts schedule
a meeting between board members and administrators. This depends on
different factors. First, some superintendents like to have these kinds of
discussions take place, while others prefer that these two groups do not
meet. This is a style issue and must be decided locally. In certain

districts the number of middle-management staff members is so large that it is somewhat cumbersome to hold this type of meeting. Consequently, we occasionally have district office personnel and/or building principals involved in these dialogues.

Regardless of approach, it is important that those involved in goal setting provide accountability for their areas of responsibility. Follow-up status reports should be planned throughout the year. As noted on the *Planning Cycle*, a midyear report by board members (subcommittee chairs) and administrators on progress toward goals is scheduled in December. If progress has been better than anticipated or problems have occurred, changes in the timelines may be adjusted.

In the spring, administrators are evaluated and further discussion between administrative staff and the superintendent takes place. At this point, progress toward goals is once again reviewed. As the school year comes to a conclusion, usually in April and May, other groups that worked on student achievement goals are asked to share their progress with the board.

GOAL MONITORING

Some districts have found it useful to develop charts that outline both instructional and management goals and who will be responsible for meeting them. The *Goal Monitoring* chart that follows provides an overview of goals and an idea of when various planning activities (Planning, Implementation, Status Reports, and Evaluation) will take place.

In addition, the makeup of each committee is listed with an asterisk next to the name of the person responsible for acting as chair. If the goal is a board of education goal, then a board member should be the chair of that group. As the chair, he or she is responsible to call meetings, see that notes are recorded and shared with the rest of the board, and provide periodic status reports. An administrator should also be assigned to each committee in order to act as a liaison to other administrators, as well as act as a resource for providing information or follow-up on requests that the committee might make.

The superintendent should not be the administrator on every sub-committee. Certainly, some goals would logically call for the superintendent's involvement; however, asking her to sit on every committee would be extremely time-consuming and would take her away from other responsibilities.[2]

Goal Monitoring

School District

BOE GOALS — instructional	Aug.	Sept.	Oct.	Nov.	Dec.	Jan.	Feb.	Mar.	Apr.	May	Jun.	Jul.	Aug.
Develop Math and Social Studies Achievement Goals K–12 *Sue, Jennifer, Hal, Principal*									P	P	P	I	I
Review Athletic Eligibility Policy *Ed, Valerie, Mike, Athletic Director*		P	P	P	S	P	P	FR					
Review Talented/Gifted vs. Enrichment Program Option *Anne, Tony, June, Principal*						P	P	P	S	P	P	FR	
Superintendent Evaluation Process *Kevin, Mary, Fred, Superintendent*		P	PI	S	P	P	FR		I				
Administrators' Goals													
Develop, Implement Curriculum Maps K–12	I	FR											
Disaggregate Midterm Exams from HS in All Involved Content Areas				P	P	I	FR						
Disaggregate State Exams from Elementary					P	P	I	FR					
Decrease Student Discipline Concerns	P	P	P	S	I	I	I	S	I	FR			

P: Planning	I: Implementation	S: Status Report	FR: Final Report

*Denotes Committee Chair

It also should be noted that the goals listed on the *Planning Cycle* do not begin in July and end in June. There seems to be a popular opinion in education that the "year" runs from July 1 to June 30. This sends an unspoken message that once a year ends, a goal is concluded. In addition, it just does not make sense that every goal should neatly fit into a twelve-month period. Some goals may be accomplished in a couple of months, but others may take a few years, particularly when focusing on something as important as student achievement.

The *Goal Monitoring* chart should also track any other stakeholder groups that develop goals. This provides all parties with an idea of what goals exist. It also allows various groups to work together in a more cohesive fashion by informing them of the direction the board and administrators have set for the district, and it provides an excellent public information tool. A copy of the *Goal Monitoring* chart can be shared in newsletters to the public to let taxpayers know that school people do in fact recognize the importance of moving toward improved performance and outcomes.

What *Shouldn't* Board Members Do to Play a Continuing Role in Improving Student Achievement?

- Probably the most important rule for board members is to remember that they are in fact board members, not administrators. This is one of the greatest threats to implementing *Focused Leadership* appropriately. An individual board member might see this as an opportunity to try to impress staff members with his or her knowledge or to try to use this as a chance to satisfy a personal concern. In certain instances, some people might try to use it to fulfill their own power needs. Any kind of behavior of this nature will alienate staff members and result in distrust.
- Board members should not contact staff members outside of the board room unless charged with doing so by a majority of the board. When the focus is on student-achievement issues, it is rare that a single board member should need to represent the entire board or the board's curriculum subcommittee. It is too easy for confusion to result or mixed messages to occur. A staff member receiving a message, whether it be a request for information or even a clarification, may not be able to accurately interpret whether the

board member is attempting to influence a decision. Since board members have a significant effect on school personnel, it is unfair to place staff members in this kind of awkward position.

- Board members should direct what might be sensitive questions to the superintendent. He in turn can provide answers or ask staff members to supply the information that is requested. By using the superintendent as a single point of entry for questions, there is greater assurance that information will be accurate and consistent.
- Board members should not evaluate staff or programs; they should evaluate their superintendent and the achievement of results. Members need to keep in mind that they are not education specialists. Although they set a strategic direction for the district, it is up to the superintendent and her staff to decide how to go about meeting the board's expectations. If goals are reasonable and have been well met, those persons responsible should be recognized and rewarded. If efforts consistently fall short and the board does not feel that outcomes are justified, then a focus on the superintendent's approach may be legitimate.

THE BOARD AND POLICY DEVELOPMENT

The primary purpose of boards of education is to set policies that administrators can use as a direction for daily operation. Although most boards will have a chapter in their policy book related to curriculum and instruction, these areas usually will not get a lot of attention. Recently, following an evening meeting in which board members and administrators worked together to discuss student achievement goals, one board member turned to us and said, "You know, I've been on the board for twelve years and this is the first time we've ever had a serious discussion about students and learning." I wish I could say this is uncommon, but in fact I have heard the same thing from almost every board I have worked with following such sessions.

Boards should review the individual policies in their handbooks in relation to the goals they have set and determine whether the policies and goals are aligned. Next, board members should develop a list of questions about how they behave as a body, which would give them an indication of whether their actions are in line with their goals and policies. An outside consultant can be useful here, since it is difficult for a board president or superintendent to lead these kinds of discussions when he or she is also a member of the group. These questions should be part of the annual self-evaluation referred to previously and should be completed by board members, as well as by the superintendent and any administrators who work closely with the board. In addition to the annual review, board members should use the policies much as a mission statement. When decisions are required, board members should be able to refer to their mission and policies to determine whether their behaviors are consistent.

A board can also provide support by adopting policies and procedures that will last beyond the tenure of any of its members (or administrators). By adopting a tool like the *Planning Cycle,* the board increases the potential that the goal-setting process will be conducted by various stakeholders in the district. Too often, a new superintendent enters a district and puts practices into place because "that's the way I've always done it." Often, these new ideas are welcome and beneficial to a district. However, where practices presently exist, no one person should have so much authority that he is able to ignore or eliminate something that has been effective in aligning goals and outcomes. In other words, when a new superintendent enters a district, conscious, intentional planning needs to take place to determine which practices will remain, which will be added, and which will be revised or eliminated.

PROVIDING FUNDING

Boards are often looked upon by staff for financial support. Making a commitment to improving student achievement does not necessarily mean that additional funds will be required. However, there may be times when extra support is needed.

One of the most important things a board can do is educate its community on where its money is going. Showing the community that the district has set serious goals and that efforts are being made to meet those goals is crucial. In the previous section it was suggested that board members review student data, as well as progress toward goals. It was also suggested that board members take responsibility for helping to develop a spirit of team effort. To show its commitment, a board should be prepared for those occasions when staff members come forward (through administration) and request extra dollars to support efforts to reach established goals. The role of staff in such cases is to show that every reasonable effort has been made to reconcile a concern and that those efforts were not successful. In addition, staff members need to be able to convince their boards that requests are likely to make substantive differences and that objective data will be gathered before and after an intervention to track and report results. As an example, using the foundation principles of *Focused Leadership: Assessment—Systems Building—Collaboration and Communication,* if a board of education is convinced (based on an *assessment* of student results) that an extra $5,000 is required to operate a summer reading program (*systems building*), the board needs to provide the support requested by staff members (*collaboration*) to operate a program for students with lagging reading scores. Finally, the superintendent needs to be sure their efforts and results are shared with appropriate stakeholder groups (*communication*).

Likewise, the board should take its role as caretaker of public funds seriously. The superintendent should provide information related to the proposed interventions that preceded the request.

- Is this intervention really necessary? If so, why?
- How were students identified?
- What strategies were used?
- What kind of evaluative data was collected?
- What options, in addition to the one being suggested, were explored and what were the advantages and disadvantages to each of them?
- What kind of data will be provided after the intervention takes place and who will be responsible for sharing that data?
- Are there services we should be eliminating in favor of others?
- Do we have data to show that present efforts are in fact moving us in the right direction?

Once again, this is a "we" effort and such questions should be voiced objectively. In fact, one board developed a list of concerns during a retreat, along with a standard list of questions that the district's educators had to complete whenever a request was being considered for funding. This has proved to be a wonderful way to educate staff members as to the kinds of issues they should be prepared to report on following the operation of a program. Likewise, it ensures that all staff members are treated similarly and that the board is not personalizing its questions toward any one individual.

PUBLIC RELATIONS

"Goals that are stated are goals that are met." This popular quote was made in response to a board member's question about why we needed to make goals public. Virtually every board we have ever worked with has voiced a concern about public relations. Too often, PR and results are considered as separate entities. Instead, boards need to look at ways to build a positive image, while at the same time getting better student results.

One superintendent from a district that is committed to improving student achievement shared a story with me, related to a member of the public who regularly came to board of education meetings for the sake of bashing the district over one financial issue or another. The superintendent finally came up with a response. He made an overhead that he brought to a board meeting. As he had anticipated, the community member got up and started complaining about costs. The superintendent (who happened to be secure in his job and secure in his person!) stood up and addressed the gentleman: "Joe, you think we spend too much on educating kids here. I'm going to show you two sets of figures. The first is our cost compared to our neighboring districts. If you look at these figures, you'll see we're in the ballpark. The second is our test results compared to similar districts from across the state. You'll see we're doing much better than most of them. You want us to do something different? You tell me what. . . . " As my colleague told me later, "Not only did he lay off, he even came up to me afterward and said he wasn't aware of that information in the past."

Education was never pushed for accountability the way it has been since the mid-1990s. Rather than avoiding this challenge, the best thing a board can do is to set clear, reasonable goals that are obtainable. Publishing these goals, along with plans on how to achieve them, is the next crucial step. One method for doing this involves developing a district portfolio that is supported by individual building portfolios. The district portfolio lists the major student achievement goals for the district and highlights the primary activities that will be used in working toward those goals. It also includes the names of stakeholders who are involved in the process. The portfolio is used by administrators and building teams as a reminder of *"where we are in relation to where we want to be."* The individual building portfolios contain data used to set goals—for instance, graphs outlining test results or survey results. District as well as building team goals might also be listed in the individual school portfolios.

This also provides the public with a sense that "they know what they're doing over there" when referring to the school board. The public often has the impression that schools merely throw money at problems with little accountability. The portfolio helps to show that real forethought and intentionality comprise a district's efforts. Portfolios are also practical tools for administrators as they share goals with staff. By being able to refer to the goals and show progress, educators have a ready frame of reference for how well they are approaching their targets.

Many districts have put portfolios to another use. Both federal and state governments place high demands on school districts for various kinds of mandated programs. Districts can use portfolios as umbrellas for sharing this information. For instance, if districts are required to have a staff-development plan in place for the state, as well as to show student progress for students with special needs, the portfolio might illustrate before and after data for students, as well as outline the staff development efforts that have (and will) take place for special education service providers.

SUMMARY

Most boards of education have focused their energies on the management side of schools rather than the educational side. *Focused Leadership* outlines specific roles for school board members. It asks board members to take responsibility for providing strategic direction to administrators and teachers by articulating student achievement goals. Once goals have been determined, board members are asked to regularly review progress and results, ensure that adequate funding exists to make sure the implementation of plans is sufficiently supported, and then see that the public is made aware of initiatives that are taking place.

While these processes are crucially important, the primary role of the board is modeling its involvement and commitment. By being public about expectations and progress and taking an active role through goal setting and review, the board sends a clear message to members of the school and community that student achievement is the district's first order of business.

NOTES

1. "Quality Counts," *Education Week,* 1999.

2. This is also an excellent opportunity for a superintendent and a board to provide opportunities for administrators to gain skills in working with boards of education. Many districts see this as a chance to provide development opportunities for central office administrators and senior principals who might aspire to higher-level administrative roles.

CHAPTER 3

The Role of Central Administration

One of the greatest abuses of time in schools involves the setting of goals that are never realized. When I first meet with school boards, I often ask if they have previously established goals. Many respond that they did develop goals in a retreat or meeting back a year or so ago. When I ask what the goals were and what kind of progress they made, it is not uncommon to hear things like:

The goals? Oh yeah, I think we made progress on them . . .
I don't really remember all of them . . .
I think the superintendent took care of them for us . . .

Obviously, there is often confusion as to who "owns" goals—or at least who is responsible for meeting goals. In many cases board members develop the goals and assume their responsibility ends at that point. Even in those cases in which board members are willing to be accountable for meeting goals, one observation that appears to be fairly consistent is that the superintendent is the most crucial person in the school district if goals are to be met. Even in the best of situations, the superintendent is key to making sure that board members have the data, personnel, and other resources they need to complete what needs to be done. More important, the superintendent is the person with the training and skills to provide leadership to the board in how to go about meeting its goals.

While the importance of modeling goal setting by the board of education cannot be understated, it is the superintendent and her central office staff that communicate the board's actions to members of the school community. The board of education relies on the central office to share goals at meetings, in newsletters, and through its regular daily routines. These staff members must regularly refer to goals when making decisions about staff development projects, hiring, and adopting new programs. In essence, the central office is key to successful implementation, and the superintendent is the one individual with the power and authority to ensure that all stakeholders are aware that these goals are of paramount importance to the district.

Using the approach described thus far, let's assume that the board of education has established and shared goals with members of the school community. Priorities and expectations have been made clear. The administrators, teachers, and support staff who work with children have a good idea of the "what." The question now is the "how."

The superintendent is the most visible individual in a school district. What he does and says is observed much more carefully than the actions of any other employee. This provides the superintendent with the opportunity to communicate to parents, teachers, and other staff members the programs that he believes are important. Superintendents who have practiced the principles outlined in *Focused Leadership* have found opportunities to initiate systems that have helped them to further student achievement results. What follows are some examples that have come from different chief school officers.

MISSION SCAN

This book started out by talking about the futility of mission statements in most districts. Certainly, if we took a hard look at *Costs vs. Results,* we might conclude that the money spent on unproductive mission statements would have achieved much greater results if used elsewhere in the instructional program. Nonetheless, some districts have taken the results of these initiatives and have actually tried to operationalize their missions and plans. Exactly how districts have done this varies. However, when done well, a carefully crafted mission statement can be an extremely valuable reference for a board, staff members, and the community.

What do school districts with effective mission statements have in common? From my observation there appears to be only one factor—a superintendent who is committed to the statement and strongly encourages and leads others to refer to it on a daily basis. This does not mean that the superintendent carries it in his pocket, printed on a card that he hands out to all he meets (though some superintendents do this). It does mean that the superintendent models the components of the mission statement and refers to it directly when it is appropriate to do so. This behavior, when successful, filters down to other staff members as well.

One way to bring the mission statement to life is through a *Mission Scan*. This breaks the statement into its component parts and asks members of the school community to dialogue on their meaning. To do this, administrators need to play a leadership role. The *Mission Scan* is an excellent means to engage in this kind of exercise.

An administrative retreat held during the summer is a good time to initiate this discussion since people are able to interact away from school in an atmosphere that may be more relaxed. In the Geneva City School District (New York) we broke the mission statement down into six component parts:

a. Safe and Healthy Learning Environment
b. High Standards of Achievement
c. Respect and Dignity
d. Open and Honest Communication
e. Varied Learning Opportunities
f. Preparation to be Members of a World Community

In this case, this was not part of a recently developed statement but one that already existed in the district prior to George Kiley's arrival as superintendent. Each administrator was asked if he or she believed that these six components were representative of the beliefs and desires of the district. There was a general consensus that the overall statement did accurately portray the values of the district and that operating in a system in which all of these were effectively in place would be very desirable. However, the administrators also agreed that they never had any discussion on what the school district would actually look like if these were in place. Nor was there a means of evaluating, through any objective method, how well each component was being operationalized. As a result, we broke into groups, with each group being asked to define one of the six components and to provide a means of measuring the extent to which each of these was being effectively practiced.

Needless to say, initial discussions pointed out vast differences in interpretations. Did a *Safe and Healthy Learning Environment* mean physically safe? Environmentally (from asbestos, lead poisoning, etc.) safe? Or psychologically safe? Were we talking about safety and health within individual classrooms? The school? On buses? Coming and returning to school, as well? Did we have responsibility for children outside of school?

Once the answers to these were settled, we had further questions: How do we know if children feel *Safe*? What measures can we use to determine a *Healthy Learning Environment?*

The outcomes to these discussions resulted in the formation of ad hoc committees at the district level to tackle several of the questions that arose, as well as to determine how to evaluate them. The committees were expected to form, do their work, and dissolve. No standing mission statement committees were enacted. Once the work was completed, the committee would lead staff members in discussions of activities that could occur in the school to complement the mission. In addition, various means of measuring the statement (surveys, observations, behavior, achievement, program data) were also identified for regular follow-up.

Although introducing the *Mission Scan* is a practical first step to take with administrators, similar follow-up conversations need to take place between administrators and their respective staffs. In addition, superintendents who use mission statements as instruments for direction often post their statements in large, readable print on board room, office, and classroom walls. I have seen superintendents point to the statement on

A group of 7–12 teachers was asked if any of them would be interested in helping to form a new middle school. After a core group was identified, its members took part in developing a mission statement for the new school. One component of the statement noted that middle school students should be segregated from high school students as much as reasonably possible (the same building houses all students, 7–12). An extra period of industrial arts ("shop") had to be taught to middle level youngsters, and so the high school shop teacher was assigned one period per day to the middle school. He informed the principal that it would be better if the middle school students came to his shop in the high school, rather than him coming over and using his colleague's room in the middle school. The middle school principal pointed to the mission statement and said that he was sorry, but his request was not in line with the school's mission.

the wall during a discussion with various stakeholders and state that the decision being made must be based on the school district's stated mission. Likewise, some superintendents will ask staff members to use the mission as a basis to challenge them if they appear to be making a decision that is in conflict with the stated mission. Some superintendents will even ask staff or board members: *How does this tie in with our mission statement?* Asking this question on a regular basis forces staff members to truly understand the spirit and meaning of the statement and to consider its importance when making recommendations.

Doing this requires a few key ingredients. One is trust. It is important that the statement is not seen as a tool for the purpose of helping the superintendent, or any other user, to meet some personal agenda. Consistency is also important. It is crucial that people share a common understanding of what the various components mean and that an educator in one building in a district would agree with a colleague in another building if faced with decisions that share similar dynamics. The purpose of this discussion is not intended to suggest what makes up a good mission statement. The point is that a well-crafted statement, developed after serious discussion, can be an important foundation for a school district.

George Kiley also used the mission statement as a tool for planning board of education agendas. Rather than using the traditional format of Regular Business, Curriculum, Buildings and Grounds, and so on, he used the components of the mission statement to guide meetings. Thus, under the topic of "Communication," which was part of the mission statement, the subtopics of Minutes, Reports, Correspondence, and Committee Matters were listed. Other mission statement components included Respect and Dignity and Members of the World Community. Board agenda items relating to reports from the assistant superintendents for Curriculum and Human Resources, the athletic director, principals, and the director of Head Start fell under these components. Mr. Kiley noted that he was fortunate to have a board president who was capable of working within this framework and that by using the mission statement in this way, the district was able to maintain it as a focal point.

PERSONNEL SYSTEMS

One of the most important things a superintendent does is hire and recommend tenure for employees. Excellent employees have a much better chance of producing students who perform in an excellent manner. Employees who lack content knowledge or who are unable to communicate effectively are not likely to produce the kind of student results that are desired. Unfortunately, many school systems do a poor job of screening and hiring teaching applicants. Schools of Educational Administration have not developed any systematic agreement on how to go about conducting the hiring process so that "best candidates" will result.

The Glens Falls, New York, schools have made a serious commitment to improving student achievement through better personnel procedures. Tom McGowan, superintendent of schools, developed a rubric with his administrators that outlined what an excellent teacher candidate should look like.

Mr. McGowan and his administrators also developed the following "Tenure Questionnaire," which principals must complete before recommending a teacher for permanent appointment. Principals are asked to complete the questionnaire and use it as a basis for reviewing candidates with Mr. McGowan and his assistant superintendent before making a tenure recommendation. The questionnaire provides a more personal view of a candidate, which increases the confidence of the superintendent in making a recommendation. It also provides principals and teachers with an idea of the expectations that are important to the district. Often, board members request a summary evaluation of candidates before voting for them. This form, along with the evaluations that took place, provides better insight to those involved in the continuing appointment and tenure process.

EVALUATION SYSTEMS

One system that is common to virtually all school systems is teacher evaluation. Systems for evaluating teachers have traditionally played an important function in determining whether individuals will be offered a continuing appointment and tenure in school districts. While the intent of teacher evaluation systems is the improvement of teacher performance, many teachers would argue that administrators often lack expertise when it comes to providing them with feedback about their instructional abilities. Often, veteran teachers argue that an administrator who was an English teacher, perhaps many years ago, lacks the content knowledge to be able to understand what is being taught in a physics classroom. In some instances, criticisms also include that the administrator doing the

Tenure Questionnaire

1. How many times have you spent twenty minutes or more in actual classroom observation of this teacher's performance?

2a. Were at least most, if not all, of your observations followed by a conference with the teacher?

2b. If so, did you gain a favorable reaction from the conferences (please provide remarks)?

3. Has anyone else been consulted on this teacher's performance? If so, provide names.

4. Has there been a significant number of student complaints, either made directly to you or relayed to you regarding this teacher? If so, how many?_____
   Comments:_____

5. Has there been a significant number of parent complaints?_____
   Comments:_____

6. Do you believe that this teacher has improved each year since beginning his or her employment with us or has performance reached a plateau?_____

7a. What have you observed in this teacher's relationship to others on the staff?_____

7b. How has he or she contributed?_____

8a. Does the teacher adequately individualize instruction?_____

8b. How does she or he help slower students?

8c. How does he or she challenge higher achievers?

9. What kind of balance did you observe in the teacher's presentation of instruction (lecture, pupil participation, etc.)? _____

10. Describe the teacher's classroom management: _____

11a. Has the teacher taken graduate study during his or her employment with us?_____

11b. Inservice?_____

11c. If provisionally certified, has the teacher given evidence of intent to become fully certified within the time limits indicated on his or her certificate?_____

12a. Has the teacher evidenced any kind of health problems that might affect his or her ability to perform effectively? _____

12b. How many days was the teacher absent in his or her first two years?_____

13a. Describe how the teacher has worked to improve student achievement:_____

13b. What data are available that will attest to his or her results?

evaluation only spent a minimal amount of time as a teacher in the class-room or that the administrator may not have had a strong reputation as an instructor himself. Sometimes the administrator is just not particularly well respected and as a result lacks credibility.

Aware that such criticisms often exist, the Orange-Ulster Board of Cooperative Educational Services (New York), which provides comprehensive special education and vocational programming for high school students and adults, decided to develop alternative methods for evaluation. The process involved the sharing of responsibility for the evaluation of teachers, along with a goal of improving student achievement. In doing this, a team of staff members developed several options in addition to traditional evaluation. These included:

1. Individual Project—a teacher may identify a special project focusing on his or her area of instructional responsibility. Projects might include activities such as staff development, independent study, or classroom research.
2. Group Project—a teacher may work on a team or in a group focusing on his or her area of instructional responsibility. Projects could include activities such as participation in study groups, classroom research, or department projects.
3. Portfolio Development—a portfolio could be developed that represents a teacher's efforts to improve student learning. The portfolio should document the concern(s) that exists, efforts made to reconcile the concern(s), and what the teacher learned as a result of his or her effort.
4. Peer Coaching—a teacher could choose to work with a skilled colleague for the purpose of mutual improvement of skills and knowledge. Each participant is required to be observed at least twice and to act as an observer at least twice.
5. Mentor Teacher/Intern or Mentor Teacher/Student Teacher Program—a teacher may act as a mentor to a new employee or student teacher to provide guidance as the individual becomes acclimated to his or her role and professional responsibilities.
6. Special Option—a staff member may work with his or her administrator in developing an effort based on special needs and interests.

The options outlined provide flexibility based on a teacher's interest, as well as on organizational need. Built into the process is a requirement that any teacher choosing one of these options must complete a short form that must be approved by his or her division administrator. More important, most of the options also require that the following *Focused Learning Proposal* form be completed, which outlines *how student achievement* will be affected.[1]

Returning again to the principles outlined in the pyramid introduced in chapter 1, *Assessment, System Building, Collaboration and Communication,* this process provides an opportunity for informative *Assessment* of instructional practice by its users; it also provides an ongoing *System* for improving student achievement and teacher skills that will remain in place even after those who constructed it leave the district. Finally, *Collaboration* is stressed between administrators and teachers in the first stage, when a choice must be made and approved. In addition, most of the options require further *Collaboration* between staff members by offering them the opportunity to work jointly on one of the options.

Focused Learning Proposal

Name of Staff Member:_____For Year:_____

Position:_____Dept.:_____

Immediate Administrator:_____Program:_____

Option Chosen:_____

1. Describe the project you have planned to undertake:
2. Which learning standard(s) does your project address?
3. What will <u>students</u> *know, be able to do,* or *believe* (for example, respect, honesty, work ethic) as a result of this project?
4. What will <u>you</u> *know* or *be able to do* as a result of this project?
5. If you are doing a project, what *steps* do you plan to take to complete it? (Use back of sheet.)
6. Are there any special *resources* (material or human) you will need to complete this project?
7. How will you evaluate your effort? (Please describe the data you will collect.)

MODELING

Nothing has a greater influence on the perceptions of staff members toward their leaders than the everyday behaviors of those leaders. When attempting to improve student achievement, it is too easy for board members and school administrators to be perceived as "ivory tower" people who are sitting over in the central office sharing edicts but not getting their own hands dirty.

If a superintendent is going to take the risk of focusing attention on student results, then it is incumbent on her to become directly involved in the implementation of the process. Some superintendents do this almost naturally. Some find it uncomfortable and as a result avoid participation. In the schools that have had the best results, the superintendent and his central office assistants are regularly observed in discussions about program efforts focused on improving achievement. They are not expected to personally know all the answers, but they do need to be seen as leaders (meaning they give support) and learners (meaning they read, and attend planning meetings, conferences, and in-services with staff).

Since accountability is one of the foundation principles in improving student achievement, the superintendent needs to model her willingness to receive feedback from staff. The *Superintendent Feedback by Administrative Staff* instrument provides a means to gather insights from those reporting to the superintendent (a similar instrument may be used by building administrators and is provided in chapter 4). As noted, it is broken down into two key domains: Instructional and Management. Each focuses on student achievement.

The instrument may be processed in a couple of different ways once completed. Immediate subordinates might be asked to complete the form and submit it to an outside consultant to be reviewed. The consultant compiles the data and then presents it to the superintendent in a summarized form. Those completing the form know ahead of time that their individual responses will not be given to the superintendent, and in some cases this may make people feel more open about their comments. The second option is to forward all surveys directly to the superintendent for personal review. Obviously, this is more efficient and ensures that the superintendent sees responses firsthand. The drawback may be less candor on the part of those completing the form. One advantage of the outside consultant is that he or she might meet with administrators after collating their data to talk with them about it. This allows the opportunity to clarify any responses that might be confusing, as well as ask for specific examples of behaviors that could help the superintendent. It is important that the discussion stay focused on the superintendent's efforts toward improving student achievement. This process is aimed at growth; it is *not* intended to be used as a superintendent's evaluation. The board is the body that is legislated to handle evaluation. The results of the feedback form go to the superintendent. In some cases, the results might be used to develop personal goals. Since the intention is growth, whether the information is shared with the board or anyone else should be the choice of the superintendent. Much of this depends on the relationship the superintendent has with her board.

While this instrument provides one means of gaining insights, there are certainly others. Some superintendents ask for feedback at the same time that they conduct evaluations of individual staff members. Some ask their administrators in a retreat setting to share their observations (some superintendents are present for this discussion, while others will excuse themselves and leave the room). I know one superintendent who periodically stands before his entire staff—administrators, instructional, and support—and says, *"I can only get better if you give me good feedback. Please write me a note telling me what I do well and where I can get better and send it to my secretary. You have my word that I will read every response."*

We know that the study of school leadership is actually a recent phenomenon. Originally, students planning to enter school administration often used the research and principles of industrial management as a basis for operating schools. As a result, the criticism that schools were (and often continue to be) run "like factories" has some merit. Probably the one most obvious difference between private and public sector leadership involves the openness that school administrators must work within. The Sunshine Laws require full, or close to full, disclosure of decision making, depending on the state[2] in which the district operates. Couple this with the movement toward public accountability, and school leaders find themselves increasingly pressured to exhibit progress toward positive results. Working within this framework of openness, the concept of accepting feedback from subordinates provides a model for others in the district to emulate. If the board of education is willing to annually self-evaluate and also take feedback from administrators, and likewise the superintendent solicits feedback from her administrators, then it seems appropriate for line administrators to ask for similar kinds of feedback from staff members (an example is

Superintendent Feedback by Administrative Staff

Scale

5: Always	3: Usually	1: Never	D: Don't Know
4: Frequently	2: Occasionally		

Please feel free to add any comments. For any scores of 1 or 2, please give specific examples.

Superintendent:_____Date:_____

INSTRUCTIONAL DOMAIN

_____ 1. Regularly focuses on administrators' instructional goals in evaluation and discussions.

_____ 2. Makes decisions that are consistent with instructional goals.

_____ 3. Provides practical suggestions and resources for solving concerns.

_____ 4. Is up-to-date and able to discuss current research.

_____ 5. Utilizes the talents and abilities of staff to ensure program effectiveness.

What does the superintendent do well in the area of instructional leadership?

_____

_____

What could the superintendent do better in the area of instructional leadership?

_____

_____

MANAGEMENT DOMAIN

_____ 6. Keeps BOE members informed and appropriately involved in instructional goals.

_____ 7. Provides opportunities for staff development that are consistent with instructional goals.

_____ 8. Encourages staff creativity and risk taking.

_____ 9. Is approachable, fair, and nonthreatening in dealing with staff.

_____10. Clearly communicates—writing, speaking, and listening.

_____11. Holds staff accountable for meeting responsibilities.

What does the superintendent do well in the area of management?

_____

_____

What could the superintendent do better in the area of management?

_____

_____

provided in the next chapter). Ultimately, we would strive to have all teachers ask for feedback from students.

REVIEWING GOALS

If indeed *What gets measured, gets done,* then it is incumbent on the superintendent to ensure that expectations are regularly reviewed. Doing this sends a crucial message—*This is so important that I am putting time in on it!*

Once goals have been established, the superintendent schedules meetings with staff members from key focus areas on a periodic basis to dialogue on efforts being made, what seems to be working, what doesn't, and what kind of help his office can provide. Staff members are asked to provide specific data and plans, as well as appropriate anecdotes. It is also important to establish dates for follow-up. The superintendent should never hold these meetings without the respective building principal in attendance. In addition, it must be emphasized that discussions are intended to be collegial and meet the *Collaboration and Communication* principles that form the foundation of the *Improving Student Achievement Pyramid.* Staff members must feel they can be honest in what they report if progress is going to be made. By learning what is working, the superintendent and staff from her office will be able to share approaches with other staff members. In order to share where progress is not being made, staff members must feel they can trust the superintendent, or they will not be likely to voice their concerns. If these concerns are not addressed, they will only perpetuate.

Joe Coleman, superintendent of the LaFayette (New York) Schools, developed a form that would be used in administrative staff and board of education meetings. The form required a response to plans that had been developed to address goals on a monthly basis. The following chart is an example of some major activities that had been established by administrators. Each administrator was aware that he or she had to give a brief update on any activity affecting their building. In those instances when an activity was not related to a particular school, it was noted with an XXX in that box. Where activities had taken place over the last month, the principal was asked to fill in the appropriate box and report out. This tool responded to the *Systems Building* principle and enhanced accountability by those

ADMINISTRATORS
Status of Follow-Up Activities

Month:_____

	ELEM SCHL 1	ELEM SCHL 2	MS / HS
STUDENT SURVEY **Principals**			Shared idea w/staff, gaining its input; Rick met with principals re: process to use to collect data. Shared expectations.
TCHR-STDT HELP AFTER SCHOOL **MS-HS Principals**	XXX	XXX	Got note to staff regarding expectations for being available, posting schedules.
2000–01 ACADEMIC GOALS — **Principals**			
MATH ACHIEVEMT. **Principals & Dept. Chair**	Kickoff 10/11	Kickoff 10/11	Kickoff 10/11
TCHRS to explain GRADING TO STDTS **MS-HS Principals**	XXX	XXX	
DEVELOP JOB DESCRIPTION FOR TCHR-TUTORS **MS-HS Principals**	XXX	XXX	Done
REVISE REPORT CARD COMMENTS **MS-HS Principals**	XXX	XXX	
NOTIFY PARENTS IF GRADE DROPS/FAILURE **Principals**			
PRINCIPALS CALL HOMES— RECOGNIZE GOOD DEEDS **Principals**			

responsible for follow-up in a timely manner. It also greatly improved communication between stakeholders.

THE ROLE OF THE ASSISTANT SUPERINTENDENT

Thus far, discussions in this chapter have referred to the superintendent. Obviously, many school districts—in fact, most—do not have an assistant superintendent. Often the superintendent must take responsibility for duties typically associated with the assistant superintendent and as a result must handle the functions related to the instructional program. Undoubtedly, this provides for a very complex and time-consuming job description.

While some districts have directors of curriculum, many ask building administrators to take responsibility within their building or even K–12. Others use consultants or share personnel with other districts. Although there is no one pattern, there is a common responsibility to serve the children in our schools. Regardless of title, the job still needs to be accomplished. For our purposes, I will refer to the "assistant superintendent" when referring to the person responsible for instructional initiatives coming out of the district office.

The following formula for improving student achievement notes that the primary ingredients are effective instruction and well-articulated curriculum that is supervised by strong leadership.

Maximum Student Achievement = Leadership + (Effective Instruction x Articulated Curriculum)

To ensure that curricular articulation occurs, a school district needs to develop a *System* to make sure that review and actions take place that focus on congruency between what is being tested and what is being taught in the schools. These should then be illustrated in the written curriculum. The movement toward standards-based programs has provided educators with a set of expectations that can be used as a comparison between what is presently being taught and tested in relation to the standards. Many districts use curriculum mapping as a process for looking at what exists in relation to what is expected. Resources explaining curriculum mapping are plentiful to educators, so we will not go into an explanation of what it is and how it might be implemented. What is important is that an effective review of curricu-lar programs takes place *on a regular basis.* Most school districts are required to conduct annual financial audits to ensure that the dollars provided by the public are properly spent. While the primary purpose of schools is to educate, most have never conducted an audit of their school program that ensures that goals and expectations are being properly met.

Administrative and board leaders often witness a great deal of turnover. As a result, it has become too easy for a new superintendent or clique of board of education members to cause the elimination of an effective practice or completely change the focus of a district's instruc-tional emphasis. The board of education needs to put a curriculum re-view process in place, preferably in board policy. The assistant super-intendent is the best person to develop and organize the implementation of curricular review. He should work with staff members to identify priority areas for consideration. Priorities should be based on factors such as student results, new curricular standards that affect the district, the adoption of new texts and instructional materials, or other related issues. Once established, each curricular area needs to be reviewed on a regular basis. Many districts choose five-year plans. Others may choose six or seven. There is no sacred number. It really becomes a matter of what local educators feel is appropriate. Also, some subjects may need review more often than others. For instance, there are a num-ber of arguments for reviewing technology on an annual or every-other-year basis, due to the rapidity with which changes are occurring. Like-wise, special education may be integrated as part of the review of each content area or as a stand-alone.

PROGRAM MANAGEMENT CYCLE

The *Program Management Cycle* shown on the next page includes a five-year review. During the first year, a series of content areas are looked at. Using this example, they include Technology, English-Language Arts, Special Education, and Health. Exactly how the review takes place may vary from district to district. Some districts develop teams that include teachers, administrators, high school students (where appropriate), and community members who may have some ex-pertise and interest in the particular area being considered. Reviews are typically conducted in relation to established local, state, or national

Program Management Cycle

Year 1: *Review and Recommend Revisions*

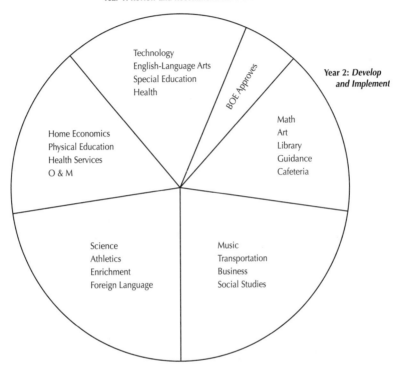

content area standards. Curriculum maps are often developed as part of this process, in order to compare what is actually being taught and tested in relation to the written curricula. Since this is a comprehensive process, at least a year needs to be set aside to complete the reviews and then make recommendations. These recommendations are then provided to the board of education for approval and implemented during the next, or second, year.

Using this model, as the technology, English-Language Arts, special education, and health areas go into their second year, a new set of content areas—home economics, physical education, health services, and operations and maintenance—start their first year. Note that health services and operations and maintenance are not instructional areas. In order to develop a culture of continuous improvement, it is important to give serious consideration to each area that contributes to the effective operation of the district. Likewise, personnel in the support areas often feel that their efforts are not as respected as the work of other people in the district. Expecting the same kind of review and high standards sends an important message that all areas, instructional as well as support, are vital parts of district operation.

SUMMARY

The role of the central office, and particularly of the superintendent, is crucial to any kind of comprehensive and meaningful change effort in the schools. Not only is the superintendent's approval important to allowing a new program or initiative to occur, but for any effort aimed at improving student achievement, her active support and involvement are imperative.

The superintendent has multiple responsibilities in this process. She must focus the district on its mission. She must act as orchestrator, publicly sharing the mission and goals that the board of education has established. Through this public behavior, she becomes a role model for administrators and other staff members in the school system.

Based on their education, training, and acumen, central office administrators must constantly identify what changes can be made in present systems, which will aid the district in determining what practices can be eliminated and what practices can be added that will help meet goals for improving student outcomes.

Perhaps one of the greatest challenges is making oneself vulnerable. If constructive feedback from subordinates is viewed as useful information for growth, then the superintendent and his staff must be willing to ask others for comments that will provide a source of meaningful data. This is especially important if other members of the organization are also going to be asked to solicit feedback from those they serve.

NOTES

1. It should be noted that a model of this form was originally developed by Sandy Keough and the administrators in the Wellsville Central Schools (New York), in an effort to provide teachers with an option to traditional evaluation.

2. Some states have full Sunshine Laws that require that all decisions be made in public, while others exempt certain areas, such as personnel and negotiations discussions.

CHAPTER 4

The Role of Building Leadership

The previous chapters described the roles played by the board of education and members of the central administration in improving student achievement. Although these groups are crucial, what happens at the building level is paramount since this is where plans must be translated into the actions that directly affect students.

This chapter is purposely titled "The Role of Building Leadership" and not "The Role of the Building Principal." While we know from the literature on effective schools that the principal plays a key role in improvement initiatives, we also know that the principal cannot be in every classroom every day, monitoring the instruction given to students. Nor can the building principal have the insights and understandings that teachers who work with students have gained through their daily contact with the children they serve. As a result, in the context of this book, building leadership really extends to all of the adults who provide instructional services to children—administrators, teachers, teacher assistants, and volunteers. Their collaboration and sharing of information are vitally important to addressing student needs.

Chapter 2 discussed the district-wide goals published by the board of education to the community. School staff has responsibility for attaining these goals and needs to discuss, by grade levels or content areas or other logical groupings, how to best go about doing so. This discussion should be outlined in action plans that act as guides for staff members.

Once plans have been developed, everyday practices need to be reviewed and modified to ensure that there is congruency between *goals* and *practices*. Staff members need to take a critical look at the common systems they engage in and often take for granted, to see if those systems can be changed to better improve achievement. For instance, school leaders need to question whether the practices they use in hiring and recommending tenure, evaluation, reporting of student grades, staff development, student discipline, budgeting, and the use of faculty meetings will move them toward the results they desire. What follows are examples of building-focused efforts that have been employed for improving student outcomes.

GOAL SETTING AT THE LOCAL LEVEL

The board of education and superintendent of one district spent more than a year discussing student outcomes and expectations. As a result, a comprehensive plan was developed that included the establishment of goals, hiring of an assistant superintendent with the specific skills to help meet the desired goals, planning of staff development, support by the board's curriculum subcommittee, and various other efforts for tracking progress.

The board's approach to setting goals in this particular district involved several meetings in which we reviewed data with its superintendent. After this initial review, the same data was shared with district administrators, along with a summary of the board's concerns. The administrative staff then engaged in serious discussion about results—how well the district had done over the last year, how the district had performed historically, as well as in relation to other districts in the area and in the state. The administrators also discussed the advantages and criticisms of the district's present testing program and how well the information they gained from the tests presently in place reflected student abilities and knowledge. The result of all this was a set of recommended goals for the board to adopt. A meeting with administrators and board members was conducted, recommendations were reviewed and revised, and goals established.

While this first step was important, the superintendent was very sensitive to the fact that even the best goals are often lost in the activity of a busy school year. Though the goals were appropriate and noble, they were of little value unless acted upon with serious intent. One way to ensure that the goals would receive appropriate attention, as well as provide a focus, was to set an expectation that the goals established by building committees reflected the strategic direction established by the board of education.

This district, like many, had building teams that were expected to identify needs and set goals. Building teams were asked to make sure that their outcomes contained the district goals that had been established (additional ones, based on specific building needs, might also be developed). Previously, building goals were defined in isolation. Each building team was allowed to develop its own, based on its perceptions of needs. Sometimes these focused on areas of student achievement, but often they addressed concerns related to department or staff needs that did not always directly deal with student achievement. The request to building administrators and leadership teams by the board and superintendent did not suggest that individual building concerns should not continue to be addressed. All they asked was that student achievement be included as primary goals at each building.

In initiating this process, the following form provided members of the building team with a clear idea of the goals expected, past results, and space to describe the strategies that the team developed to address the goals. Space was also provided for benchmarks that could be used to determine progress. This format is grounded in all of the foundation concepts provided at the base of the *Improving Student Achievement* pyramid: it calls for a *System,* which requires discussion by staff; it includes an *Assessment* component, using objective data from past results; it also requires *Collaboration* by staff in order to develop building-wide plans; and listing the information for forwarding to the board of education meets the need for *Communication.*

While the board's goals remained the same, variations occurred on how these forms were completed, based on factors such as grade levels or school organization. For instance, where the elementary school had two or three *Focus Areas,* the secondary schools asked staff in each content area to develop at least one student achievement goal. As an example, the social studies department may be looking to improve the percentage of students who pass U.S. History in grade 11, as well as to improve the percentage who score at distinction level in Global Studies. Likewise, where a building team may respond to goals at the elementary level, it may be more appropriate due to the organization of schools for departments to develop goals at the secondary levels. What is important is that all of the staff members with direct involvement in delivering instruction to children take part in discussion and planning. Unless these key people feel that the goals have value and are important, it is unlikely that any extra effort will be made to reach them.

GOALS

The ABC Board of Education is committed to seeing that:

a. Student achievement on all state assessments will be greater than regional and similar schools.

b. Student achievement on all state assessments will be greater than the average scores of students from the previous three years.

c. Student achievement on the MAT will result in 100% of students gaining at least one year's growth in reading and math.

d. By 2000–2001, 80% of students will score at or above the Distinction level on state tests.

e. By 2002–2003, the high school will rank in the top 150 high schools in NYS in Regent's performance.

FOCUS AREAS

Elementary School A

Math

ELA

Science

MEASUREMENTS

Area: Test-Rdg 3	Test-Math 3	Test-Wrtg 5
1996: ___	___	___
1997: ___	___	___
1998: ___	___	___
1999: ___	___	___

Area: Test-Rdg 6	Test-Math 6	Test-Wrtg 6
1996: ___	___	___
1997: ___	___	___
1998: ___	___	___
1999: ___	___	___

DATA: TEACHER BY TEACHER

Once goals have been set, it is imperative that ongoing *Assessment* take place. Administrators and teachers must acknowledge how well students are performing in relation to the goals that have been established and then determine what additional resources and training will be required to allow teachers to move students toward these desired goals. In order to do this, building staff need to identify multiple means for assessing student progress.

Historically, educators have relied heavily on subjective measures, which included certain beliefs and values that individual teachers bring to scoring when judging student progress. Two studies of student grading that received a great deal of attention were conducted as long ago as 1912 by Starch and Elliott.[1] In one study they sent two English papers written by two students to 200 high schools and asked first-year English teachers to grade the papers. Papers were graded on a percentage from zero to a top score of 100. Of the 142 schools responding, the variation for the first paper ranged from 64 to 98 and for the second, 50 to 97. One paper was given a failing grade by 15 percent of those doing ratings, while 12 percent gave a grade of 90 or better. For those who believed that English was too subjective, Starch and Elliott[2] conducted a second study involving papers in geometry. In this study the variation of 138 papers that were returned was even greater, with scores on one paper ranging from 28 to 95.

Some results of efforts from researchers who looked at grading led to further attention to grading policies. A study by Page[3] (1958) looked at papers that were returned to students that included teacher comments. Page found that those students who received standard comments such as "Excellent! Keep it up" at the high end and "Let's bring this up" or "Let's raise this grade!" at the low end performed significantly better than those who did not receive any comments. They also found that those students who received personalized or individual comments scored even better. Page concluded that grades can affect student learning when accompanied by teacher comments.

As a result of what research has taught us, we need to use various means to judge how students are performing. Schools that have made improvements in student achievement a goal have used several different approaches to do this.

Some secondary schools have required that all staff members give quarterly or midterm examinations that are the same for all students in a given subject area. For instance, the *English Midterm Analysis* is an

BUILDING/GRADE-LEVEL BENCHMARKS

SCHOOL-BASED TEAM STRATEGIES

example from one school in which four different teachers provide instruction in tenth-grade English. This is a relatively large high school and ten sections of this course are offered. To ensure that the level of difficulty is similar, test questions all came from state tests from past years and each teacher gave the same midterm exam. This ensures that one teacher's test is not easier than his colleagues'. In the example provided, results are broken down by those receiving a grade of 54 of less, 55 to 65, 65 to 84, and 85 to 100. Finally, the *Total Students* (total number of students for each section), *# Failing* (the number failing), and the *% Failing* (percentage of those failing the test) are also listed. In this particular school there is also a gender (*M/F*) breakdown. Scores can be disaggregated through virtually any means the district desires. For instance, ethnicity might be used since this is an area of concern in schools with diverse populations.

It should be noted that the English teachers whose results are outlined on the following chart used questions that came from old exams covering the entire year. Thus, it was anticipated that scores would be low since students would be tested in January and many items had not yet been covered in their classes. However, the teachers were using this both as a means of determining how much students had learned about the content that had already been reviewed, as well as to identify how much they already knew about content to be covered.

Another school district disaggregated elementary student results using *those students who used a computer-based program* for the delivery of part of their math instruction. The superintendent asked about half of the elementary teachers in a building if they would use the computer-based system with their students for at least fifteen minutes per day, per student. He said he would place three computers in each of their classrooms so that students would have immediate access. At the conclusion of the year the results were graphed by teacher and grade level. Those students whose teachers used the computers made significant jumps compared to nonusers. As a result, in the following year computers were placed in Title I classrooms, and students improved so dramatically that almost half of the students tested out of the Title I program. The following chart was shared with the board of education and staff members to help illustrate results that were gained.

The key in both of these examples is that results have been broken down, teacher by teacher. Doing this will raise "red flags" with some staff members, since many people fear the concept of accountability and are threatened by it. Once again, it is important that the principle of *Collaboration* be emphasized and that the message be sent that all of

ENGLISH MIDTERM ANALYSIS

Teacher	Period	<54 M	<54 F	55–64 M	55–64 F	65–84 M	65–84 F	85–100 M	85–100 F	Total Stdts M	Total Stdts F	# Failing M	# Failing F	% Failing M	% Failing F
Tchr 1	4	2	0	2	2	3	3	3	3	10	8	4	2	40%	25%
	6	1	1	1	1	2	4	2	5	6	11	2	2	33%	18%
	Total	4		6		12		13		35		10			29%
Tchr 2	6	3	1	1	2	5	4	2	0	11	7	4	3	36%	43%
	7	3	2	1	2	3	5	0	1	7	10	4	4	57%	40%
	Total	9		6		17		3		35		15			43%
Tchr 3	1	3	2	3	2	3	3	1	0	10	7	6	4	60%	57%
	5	3	1	1	2	7	3	0	0	11	6	4	3	36%	50%
	8	3	1	3	5	2	2	2	0	10	8	6	6	60%	75%
	Total	13		16		20		3		52		29			59%
Tchr 4	2	0	0	2	0	4	3	4	3	10	6	2	0	20%	0%
	3	2	0	0	1	4	3	0	2	6	6	2	1	33%	17%
	5	1	1	3	1	2	6	2	2	8	10	4	2	50%	20%
	Total	4		7		22		13		46		11			24%
Total English	All (M)	21		17		35		16		89		38		43%	
	All (F)		9		18		36		16		79		27		35%
	Total	30		35		71		32		168		65			39%

65 (39%) | 103 (61%)

In one district that used the *Midterm Analysis*, the superintendent relayed that a teacher was up for tenure during the year that this format for reviewing data was used for the first time. An item analysis indicated that her students did not fare well on content taught prior to giving the midterm. This kind of analysis had not been used before, and the results caused the superintendent to review the teacher's progress in previous years. The superintendent shared that he had mixed feelings—the teacher was popular, appeared to be conscientious, and was motivated. However, results were not up to par with expectations. The superintendent's question to the principal was: *Is she failing the district, or did we fail her?* He was concerned that perhaps she was not given enough attention and assistance as a new teacher, and the district had fallen short in providing the help she needed. Ultimately, he did not make a tenure recommendation for that year but struck an agreement with the teacher and her union to extend her probationary period for a year. During that time, she was given additional mentoring and support and ultimately was granted tenure a year later, a stronger teacher.

us can improve, successes and failures are shared by all stakeholders, and the primary purpose for reviewing data in this way is for problem solving and improvement.

Breaking down data by staff member is vital if we wish to improve student outcomes. The process for doing this must consider all kinds of factors that affect results. If one teacher has been assigned a larger number of low-achieving students, he cannot be fairly compared to his colleagues without controlling for this. Likewise, if a teacher in one building averages fifteen students in her eighth-grade English classes and another eighth-grade English teacher averages twenty-five students, comparisons may not be legitimate. Furthermore, many people in education will attest to the fact that in some years total grades are stronger or weaker academically than in others. It is important to keep such factors in mind. It is also important to keep data over a period of time and not make decisions based on one year's results. Finally, it is wise to collect different kinds of data from various sources before drawing any conclusions.

The first example outlined in the following section, "Teachers/Three Years' Results on Grade 5 Writing Rubric," provides three years of

Comparison of Users–Nonusers of Computers for Math Instruction

	Computers Used 15 Min. Day/per Stdt.	Traditional drill— Stations, Teacher Monitoring
Students Scoring at Levels 1 or 2	15.9% N: 14	39% N: 32
Students Scoring at Levels 3 or 4	84.1% N: 74	60.9% N: 50

results of four teachers who used the same assessment tool. In this case, students were randomly and equitably grouped, based on achievement. Listing both raw scores and percentages provided different ways of looking at the results gained over the three years. A review shows that the results from Teacher 1 have consistently improved in each of the three years. Results from Teachers 2 and 3 have been consistent, though Teacher 3's may be less than acceptable. Teacher 4, obviously, has shown significant improvement with each administration. While this data is helpful in getting one view of how each of these teachers' students have performed on a particular test, it does not provide any information on how the same students performed on other assessments or which of their skills were strengths. Consequently, when making judgments about student performance, it is important to use multiple sources of data and information. The following Writing Rubric provides three years' worth of results for four different teachers.

Teachers/Three Years' Results on Grade 5 Writing Rubric

Rubric	TCHR 1	TCHR 2	TCHR 3	TCHR 4
5	7/9/8	9/7/8	5/4/5	3/6/8
4	6/7/8	6/7/7	7/5/7	7/7/7
3	4/2/2/1	2/2/0	4/6/3	3/3/2
2	2/1/1	2/1/2	2/3/4	4/2/2
1	2/1/0	0/2/1	3/3/2	4/1/0
5-4-3	81%/90%/94%	89%/84%/83%	76%/71%/71%	62%/84%/89%
2-1	19%/10%/6%	11%/17%/17%	24%/29%/29%	38%/16%/11%

Another approach to looking at data involves a breakdown by program categories. In this example, the outcomes of students with Limited English Proficiency, students receiving Title I services, and students coming from special education are provided.

Instrument: <u>Math or ELA Test and Special Support</u>

Rubric	LEP	Title I	Spec Ed
4	8	5	3
3	9	9	6
2	2	4	2
1	2	6	3
4–3	17	14	9
2–1	4	10	5

In this example, the Pass/Fail rates of three teachers on a state examination are outlined.

Instrument: <u>Report Card Pass-Fail & Regents</u>

State Math Exam

	Tchr 1		Tchr 2		Tchr 3	
	P	F	P	F	P	F
85–100	12	2	7		3	
65–84	25	6	9	1	14	1
55–64	8	7	2	2	11	5
<54	3	8	1	3	4	7

One of the most useful tools for following results comes from a superintendent who developed a ten-year record of every teacher in the school district. The following is an edited example of an English teacher's results (note, this teacher did not teach Math 10 between 1990 and 1994).

The superintendent using this format finds it to be a valuable tool. Staff members are asked to review their own data and share their observations with their supervisor. Where performance is consistently below an acceptable level (passing is considered to be 65 percent), teachers and administrators work together to develop a plan for improvement. Data from other local districts, as well as other districts in the state, are often accessible to those teachers who are interested in reviewing it for comparison purposes.

Once again, it is important to keep the foundation principles in mind when using data: *Assessment, System Building, Collaboration and Communication.* Numbers are often intimidating and teachers may feel that they are being singled out when results are poor in comparison to the benchmarks that have been identified. It is important that school leaders emphasize, when first using such tools, that student *Assessment* is a crucial core component of the curricular program and good data is necessary in order to plan and make changes that are necessary. It is also important to incorporate approaches or *Systems* that are informative and result in improvement. Finally, if staff members are going to be open about what is working and what is not, administrators must develop their own personal track records over time for being *Collaborative* and not punitive in the way they view and act on information.

INSTRUCTIONAL DELIVERY

Probably no job is more difficult or challenging than that of a teacher. Most educators are good people who work hard at providing opportunities for growth to their students. The role of teachers has typically been a fairly isolated one. While schools are actually highly social places, and opportunities are structured through means such as faculty room spaces, staff meetings, and staff development programs, teachers have historically conducted planning and teaching activities in isolation.

The new environment of high stakes testing that has been placed on educators requires them to share ideas and approaches that are effective in order to improve student outcomes. Furthermore, it is the primary responsibility of school administrators to take the lead in efforts to enhance collaboration that will lead to real, tangible results.

Math 10—Smith	90–91	91–92	92–93	93–94	94–95	95–96	96–97	97–98	98–99	99–00
% Passing Exam					71	74	61	76	88	84
% Pass Exam w/85+					9	8	8	9	15	25
% Failing Exam					29	26	39	24	12	16
# Enrolled					48	46	45	47	23	24
% Passing Course					83	78	67	81	91	92
% Passing w/85+					5	6	4	5	7	5
% Failing Course					17	22	33	19	9	8

The *Student Education Plan* that follows is a good example of the *Assessment, Systems Building, Collaboration and Communication* principles and has been used by principals and teachers as a means of focusing on specific student needs. The *Plan* can be used with an individual student or small groups of students within a teacher's room.

Assessment

For example, the principal of a building might regularly schedule brief meetings with each teacher to review the progress of students who are not performing as expected (not only low achievers but "high flyers," who should be doing above average but are not). The teacher would be asked which students in her fourth grade class were performing below expectations in Language Arts. The teacher shares the names of nine students. The principal asks some questions. The first one requires the teacher to be able to be objective about how he determined students' needs: *How did you assess (or determine or know) these kids are having problems?* The teacher should be able to articulate how the need was identified and be able to share it.

The principal then asks what kinds of specific problems the students are having. The teacher might reply that four are having difficulty with reading comprehension problems, three with listening assignments, and two others with processing information from reading.

Collaboration

The teacher is then asked to share what he has done with these students thus far to address their deficiencies and what resulted. The teacher is also asked if he has any other ideas for approaches that might be useful with this group. At this point, the principal's role as instructional leader becomes important. The principal should be able to share other ideas or approaches that the teacher might use. The principal is expected to be the best-read and most up-to-date resource in the building, in terms of educational literature. She should be able to refer to approaches she is aware of from reading articles or books or from her own experiences.

It is important to be as specific as possible about needs and remedies. It is also important that the principal and teacher follow up on any plans. The *Student Education Plan* is a tool to help organize information on individuals and small groups of children. One teacher commented that "This is kind of like the IEP (Individual Education Plan) that we use in Special Ed." In fact, it is but without the bureaucratic requirements. It requires reflection and collaboration and calls on the principal and teacher to be accountable to try some new approaches and then assess and report back on their progress.

A reasonable period of four to six weeks should take place from the development of the *Plan* to the time that the principal and teacher meet again to assess their efforts. If progress is being made, the *Plan* should be continued and another meeting set up in another four to six weeks. If progress is not being made with some or all of the students, the principal should be able to refer the teacher to resources at other schools or other colleges, universities, or other educational support organizations in the area. Finally, if the principal is not aware of any specific sources, she should be ready to make contact with someone in the district office, such as the assistant superintendent, to ask for further assistance.

Systems Building

The *Student Education Plan* provides a simple system for ensuring attention to students who are not performing as expected. It requires honest assessment with a focused response by teachers and administrators. It helps to ensure that every student is given every reasonable opportunity to be successful and those efforts are well documented and have been planned in an educationally sound manner. In addition, the *Student Education Plan* is a good way to ensure a systematic approach on the part of teachers and principals to be sure that all students are receiving appropriate attention in a timely manner.

Communication

The *Student Education Plan* also provides a history on students, which might be useful to teachers from year to year. For instance, if the eighth-grade science teacher is not having success with a student, she

---

Student Education Plan

Teacher:_____Grade/Course:_____Date:_____

Student(s):

Performance Concerns:

Efforts to Date:

Efforts to Try (Resources Needed?):

Next Meeting Date:

---

would be able to check the student's records to identify his previous teachers. These teachers may well have had similar concerns and discovered approaches with this student that provided some success. With the magnitude of demands now placed on teachers, it is not reasonable to expect every teacher to remember in detail what he did to deal with every poorly performing student. This *Plan* provides a written history that may be of value. The *Plan* can also be a useful communication device to use with students and parents. It may be appropriate to let both students and parents know that this kind of discussion is taking place—that learning is important to the staff in the school and a special effort is being made to give this individual student personalized support.

The following came from one superintendent:

We adapted the *Student Education Plan* in order to get a number of fourth-graders through the state's English-Language Arts test and the state's Math test. We have an aide working with all students who scored below level on the preliminary test. She actually sat down with each student, one on one, and showed them the *Student Education Plan.* She reviewed the specific areas in which they were weak on their preliminary test and gave them examples of the kinds of things that they were going to receive help in.

We developed a bank of parallel tasks and scheduled these kids on a regular basis for extra help. Two weeks before the actual test we also provided them with additional daily tutoring. Out of the four elementary schools in the district, this building had the best results. What's more amazing is that this building also has a significantly larger special education population and these students were included in the results.

WORKING WITHIN THE STANDARDS-BASED CURRICULUM

Other examples involve teachers and administrators working together to determine the kinds of skills and knowledge their elementary grade students need in order to be successful in dealing with standards-based programming.

The traditional method of curriculum development in schools follows a process in which teachers decide what they want students to know and be able to do.[4] Theoretically, the curriculum guide is then implemented and assessment takes place, again following what was outlined in the curriculum guide. In reality, it is not uncommon to enter a school and ask a teacher for a copy of a curriculum and receive a blank stare. While curriculum guides may or may not exist, they have never become strong frameworks for what actually happens in most classrooms. In fact, experience tells us that textbooks have the greatest impact on determining curriculum content.

With standards-based programming taking place in what has become known as a "high-stakes environment," due to public reporting required of schools, many educators have felt forced to alter the traditional curriculum process. For many, curriculum development now requires starting at the end, with assessment, and then developing the implementation (instructional) phase, followed by writing the curriculum guide. This change is illustrated by Dr. William Silky:

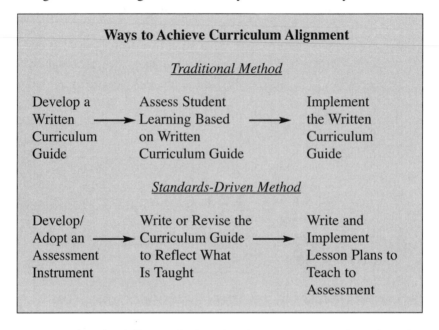

Ways to Achieve Curriculum Alignment

Traditional Method

| Develop a Written Curriculum Guide | → | Assess Student Learning Based on Written Curriculum Guide | → | Implement the Written Curriculum Guide |

Standards-Driven Method

| Develop/ Adopt an Assessment Instrument | → | Write or Revise the Curriculum Guide to Reflect What Is Taught | → | Write and Implement Lesson Plans to Teach to Assessment |

Addressing the delivery of educational programs to students in order to maximize results again follows the principles of *Focused Leadership*.

Assessment

In one district, the principal and teachers decided that it was important for them to have an understanding of what was expected of students who would be administered the Language Arts examination by the State Education Department.

Collaboration & Communication

In order to prepare for this, a group of teachers worked with the principal in doing an analysis of the content and skills that were required to perform well on this test. Once they completed this analysis, they broke these down into categories based on the three areas emphasized on the test: Reading Comprehension, Listening/Writing, and Reading and Gathering Information.

This *Collaboration* experience was so practical and useful that it continued to be used for all of the other content areas as well. Not only did it allow for *Communication* between teachers at grade levels but also for communication of teachers *between* grade levels.

Systems Building

Once the analysis was completed, a number of examples were developed that could be shared with all teachers in the building for use in their daily lesson planning. This was also helpful to the principal, who was able to use it as a frame of reference in speaking with staff members about what was being done in classrooms, as well as during observations, walk-throughs, and the reviewing plans. The analysis and examples outlined in the following chart were only the first step. Once teachers shared this initial effort, fellow staff members from throughout the building developed further exemplars that were shared with colleagues. This helped to ensure that all faculty members spoke and taught using a common language. It also helped improve communication by allowing staff members to know more about other matters related to instruction, such as the amount of time being spent in various content areas and the levels of expectation that colleagues had for their students.

What we learned, quite simply, is that another way of gathering useful information for improving student achievement is by asking people.

Assessment

The following instrument was developed[5] as part of an overall effort in districts to determine whether information and resources were being appropriately channeled. This survey was given to both teachers and administrators, and a simple comparison was completed. The purpose of the survey was *not* to identify who was doing the "right" or "wrong" thing but rather to get an idea of whether stakeholders believed they were well informed and knowledgeable about program-related information.

LANGUAGE ARTS ANALYSIS

Section I: Reading Comprehension	Section II: Listening/Writing	Section III: Reading and Gathering Information
Multiple Choice Questions • Main Idea or Theme: be able to identify. • Motivation: Why did a character act as he or she did? • Context clues: to determine what words mean. • Predict: How might a character act in another situation?	Writing assignments • Quotes: explain the meaning of quotes found in passages. • Phrases: explain their use. • Lessons learned: explain the lessons learned from a folk tale. • Give an example of something that was learned from a lesson.	Writing assignments • Details: identify details from context. • Give examples of details from context that support a statement. • Conclusions: provide conclusions coming from graphic organizers. • Assimilate information from two different stories.

EXAMPLES TO USE WITH STUDENTS

Reading Comprehension	Listening and Writing	Gaining Information from Reading
• What is the main idea? • Why did the main character behave as she did? Base your argument on information you gathered from the story. • Based on what was said, what do you think [vocabulary word] means? • How do you think the character would have acted if his dog had lived instead of died?	• Explain this quote: • Give a phrase from the story and explain what it meant. • What is the moral of the story? • Share something that has happened to you that is similar to what happened to the main character and what you learned from it.	• What led to the character's leaving his best friend on the mountain? (Give details from the story.) • Make an argument and support it using details from the story. • Develop and explain each stage of a graphic organizer from start to end. • Share and explain a conclusion using events from two different stories.

Program Audit Standards

Respond to the statements below using the following scale. Please provide an explanation for any response scored at 1 or 2 (use the back if necessary).
1: Strongly disagree 2: Somewhat disagree 3: Agree 4: Somewhat agree
5: Strongly agree

_____ 1. The local curriculum is aligned with state standards and assessments.

_____ 2. There is an ongoing effort to update staff of changes in state-level curriculum (standards documents, resource guides, tests, etc.).

_____ 3. Staff members who are responsible for delivering curriculum are made aware of changes to local curriculum.

_____ 4. There is adequate supervision of the curriculum, and principals/supervisors monitor fidelity to the written/tested curriculum.

_____ 5. Financial and other resources are adequate to ensure that the curriculum is aligned.

_____ 6. The curriculum shows evidence of attention to students' developmental levels.

_____ 7. The curriculum accounts for current and future social trends.

_____ 8. The curriculum is based upon sound learning theory.

_____ 9. The curriculum is balanced and relevant.

_____ 10. There are adequate instructional materials (textbooks, computers, equipment, etc.) to support implementation of the curriculum.

_____ 11. There is consistency between teacher-made and standardized assessments.

_____ 12. Student performance data are regularly used to inform instruction.

_____ 13. Program and building administrators regularly work with teachers to analyze student performance data.

_____ 14. New strategies are developed to improve student performance.

_____ 15. Teachers at each grade level share ideas and materials.

Systems Building

If the survey is given on an annual basis, principals and curriculum supervisors should be able to gain useful information on how well they have been able to keep constituent staff members informed and updated on program-related matters. This format also helps clarify the expectation that the central office may have of its administrators and is a useful tool to provide to new administrators.

> **Collaboration &
> Communication**

In using a survey like this, it is important to disaggregate the information gathered by unit. The unit will typically be by school or department. If one principal does a very comprehensive job of getting and sharing information and another does not, then the latter needs to know what expectations exist and be offered help, if needed, in making sure staff members are better informed in the future.

SUMMARY

No matter how well intentioned a board of education or superintendent may be, unless the principals and teachers who work with students on an everyday basis are committed to an idea, it will not be effective. For that matter, the powerful role of "teacher as decision maker" is exercised every day in every classroom. Once the door closes on a teacher and his class, he has almost free choice as to what will happen.

Teachers have not been given clear direction over the years in many school districts about curricular expectations. The present emphasis on accountability has changed that. Educators are much more aware of what is expected of them as a result of testing and reporting than they ever were before.

Where boards and central office administrators can make a difference is in supporting the needs of faculties as they, in turn, work to meet the needs of students. To do this, it is crucial that school boards, administrators, and faculty in the schools clearly understand the goals and expectations that they hold for students.

Once outcomes are understood, building staff members must be willing to take a critical look at what they do and the kinds of results their efforts are providing. The use of objective, disaggregated data for the purpose of planning cannot be understated. It is imperative that those who deliver programs to students clearly understand how each child has been affected by his or her classroom experience.

Once school personnel have a clear idea of what belongs in the curricular program and which instructional practices are most effective, they will then be prepared to develop appropriate materials, plan staff development programs, and review the various other systems that are in place to make sure that what they do is aligned with where they want to be.

This commitment and follow-up must be embedded in the principles outlined in the strategies shared in this and previous chapters: *Assessment* that is honest and unbiased, *Systems Building* that is an ongoing part of the process and will survive turnover in personnel, *Collaboration* that is focused on improving academic outcomes, and *Communication* that provides a forum for sharing what works and what does not work.

NOTES

1. Starch, D., and E. C. Elliott. (1912). "Reliability of the Grading of High School Work in English." *School Review* 20: 442–457.

2. Starch, D., and E. C. Elliott. (1912). "Reliability of the Grading of High School Work in Mathematics." *School Review* 21: 254–259.

3. Page, E. B. (1958). "Teacher Comments and Student Performance: A Seventy-Four Classroom Experiment in School Motivation." *Journal of Educational Psychology* 49: 173–181.

4. This refers to the "written curriculum" handed to new teachers and usually followed a combination of textbooks, national, state, and local recommendations. It does not include the taught curriculum (what was actually taught) or the tested curriculum (what was actually tested).

5. The *Program Audit Standards* survey was developed by Dr. William Silky and myself as an informal tool to be used to gather information in districts subscribing to *Focused Leadership* initiatives.

CHAPTER 5

Getting Started

As noted throughout this book, *Focused Leadership* provides a number of options for implementation. The local environment should determine how much can be done and how quickly. However, this should not be used as an excuse to fail to improve the educational program for students. School leaders, and this includes members from each of the groups that have been highlighted—board members, administrators, and teachers—all have a responsibility to see that the children being served receive the most effective program possible. Some of the typical barriers to change—petty politics, unwillingness to try new ideas, and personal comfort—have to be put aside in favor of better meeting the needs of children. At times it will be necessary for those adults in positions of authority to make decisions that will be unpopular. Change is not always embraced and doing so takes courage.

The following descriptions will provide suggestions for school districts interested in using the principles of *Focused Leadership* to improve student achievement. Much of what is outlined will have been described, at least in part, in prior chapters. The purpose here is to provide some ideas of how to get started, options that might exist at each stage, and a sequence for implementation.

FIRST STEPS

The board of education and superintendent are crucial to initiating *Focused Leadership*. The most important role for each is modeling. People in the school district need to see that members of the board and the superintendent are genuinely committed to improving student achievement, and the most powerful indicator of this is how they behave on a daily basis. The adage "Walking the talk" is most appropriate. Examples abound of people in leadership positions saying that learning is the number one priority. Unfortunately, too often actions contradict this statement, resulting in skepticism by those working in the schoolhouse each day.

The first step in the process requires board of education members to confirm their commitment to the goals and principles involved in *Focused Leadership*. Board members need to understand the implications of the model and actively support the efforts that will be made to improve student achievement. Board members also need to agree to do business differently than they have in the past.

OPTIONS FOR MEETINGS

In order to get started, the board of education and superintendent should spend at least eight to ten hours discussing present and desired student achievement. Typically, a Friday evening/Saturday or two evenings are sufficient. Meetings should not be as formal in nature as regular board of education meetings. Ideally, a retreat setting is best so that materials can comfortably be passed around, shared on overheads or through computer presentations, and used for discussion. Since student achievement data are being shared, it is quite possible that individual teachers may be identified in the course of discussion (for instance, if talking about the results of the physics program, it may be rather obvious who the instructor is since there is only one person teaching physics). Consequently, if possible, the retreat setting is preferable. If the meeting must be held in a forum that is open to the public, then it should be stressed that specific personnel will not be referred to in discussion.

A facilitator should be used so that the superintendent can participate in the discussions. It is important that all board members be present, as well as the superintendent. The assistant superintendent (or equivalent) in charge of curriculum and instruction should also attend. It is not necessary to have building administrators or other staff present during these initial discussions.

These meetings provide an opportunity to talk about the principles of *Focused Leadership: Assessment, Systems Building,* and *Collaboration and Communication.* The implications of these principles in practice need to be stressed. For instance, by sharing *Assessment* data, districts will be better able to identify where students are performing well or poorly. Looking at data from a variety of sources and over a period of time will help educators and administrators point out where districts need to concentrate efforts for improvement in the future. It is also important here to be sensitive to interpersonal issues. Those staff members who have responsibilities in low-performing areas may become defensive and unwilling to cooperate in trying new ideas. As a result, emphasizing a culture of *Collaboration* is crucial. Board members must stress, through both their words and actions, that this is a team effort and success is a result of all parties working together. When student performance is not up to expectations, the team also has the responsibility to develop new *systems* that will help improve performance.

SETTING GOALS

Once a climate of *Collaboration* has been established, the board of education is responsible for setting goals. As noted previously, different approaches can be used to do this, and all of these have been used with success. No one method would work in all districts. It is important that the superintendent be able to gauge the political climate in the school community. She needs to know how change efforts are likely to be accepted, based on factors such as the labor relations history of the district; the personalities of the individuals who speak for the teachers (this may be the union leadership but not always); the skill level of her administrators, as well as her own ability to get acceptance from staff; and the urgency of the needs being addressed.

- In District A the teacher leadership was receptive to trying new ideas and, if the superintendent could provide reasonable evidence of a need, would typically go along with a proposal. Negotiations could be challenging but were always respectful, and the trust level was high as a result of a number of years of consistent behavior on the part of leadership from both labor and management. Likewise, the board and superintendent were confident that children really were the first priority of all groups involved. In this district the board met by itself several times and ultimately voiced two concerns: first, a desire to raise student performance outcomes and, second, to improve the image of the district in the geographic area in order to draw people, particularly people concerned about the educational program who would contribute to the district. The board believed that one goal would complement the other. While the board had these discussions, the superintendent called building administrators together and they were provided with the same data the board was reviewing. Administrators were asked to share their views and recommendations. Once they did this, a joint meeting was held with board members and administrators. The outcome of the meeting was a set of specific student achievement goals that the superintendent shared with all teachers. Because of the healthy climate in the district, the board and superintendent were able to then share the goals with the public that they had identified and to begin the implementation phase of their effort.

- In District B, the administrators spent time in a couple of staff meetings in the spring to talk about the kinds of data that would be useful in setting goals and also reviewed data from recent years. During a full-day summer retreat, recently generated data from the end of the previous school year was used as a basis for recommendations to the board. These were accepted and then shared with staff. Again, a relatively high degree of trust existed within the district, and once the goals were shared, further planning for implementation took place.

- The culture in District C called for collaboration between instructional staff and administrators before recommendations were made to the board. In this case the board accepted the concept and principles involved in *Focused Leadership* and decided that the goal-setting process should start at the grass-roots level with the staff members who deliver the program. As a result, in this district discussions took place between principals and teachers, recommendations were shared with administrators, and ultimately goals were taken to the board of education. Board members then reviewed the goals and made some minor adjustments prior to their adoption. This district did not have a poor labor relations environment; however, historically the decision-making process called for direct involvement by faculty on any matters involving instruction.

MAKING GOALS PUBLIC

Regardless of the method used, once goals have been established, they need to be made public.

- The first step involves sharing goals in the school district. This may be done by either the superintendent or building administrators going to the faculty in each building and outlining the goals that were adopted. While we have seen both approaches used, the impact of the superintendent standing before a faculty and advocating the importance of raising student achievement and stating his support for collaboration by all staff in reaching goals can be very powerful. It also sends a clear message about the priority being given to this effort since superintendents do not commonly make these kinds of appearances before staff.
- In addition to sharing goals within the district, this information should also be provided to the community. As a way of further encouraging accountability, this kind of public declaration of intentions puts everyone directly involved—board members, administrators, teachers, aides, parents, and students—on notice that a commitment has been made to the public and that everyone needs to contribute to make this it a reality. Sharing with the public also lets it know that its board is operating in a responsible, corporate manner. As with excellent companies, its school district is run based on sound planning and not serendipity. The sharing of goals may be done through a district newsletter, as well as through declarations on boardroom and office walls within the district.

IMPLEMENTING

Once goals have been developed, the next step involves taking action. A well-used adage tells us: "Do the same thing today that you did yesterday, and you can expect to get the same results tomorrow." We also know from experience that asking people in schools to change their behavior is one of the most difficult challenges for school leaders.

The publicizing of goals should put everyone on notice that a serious effort has been initiated. Some veterans of failed initiatives may see this as yet another fad that will come and go, so it is important that real, substantive actions take place. This should occur at various levels within the district. In getting started, the superintendent should take leadership in identifying actions that fall into two categories: those that the system can handle *immediately,* and those that can be implemented immediately but will take *a period of time* to complete and require collaborative planning.

IMMEDIATE ACTIONS

First, the board, superintendent, and administrators should take a look
at various strategies that might be implemented on short notice.

- For instance, one superintendent made it clear to all staff that
  midterm examinations would be given in every academic content
  area in the high school. Furthermore, the midterms would be the
  same for each section of a common course (in other words, every
  tenth-grade social studies teacher would use the same examination).
- The high school principal in one district determined that it would be
  reasonable to ask all staff giving midterm examinations to disaggregate midterms and finals to determine in which areas students did
  well or poorly and develop a plan to deal with areas of below standard performance (see English Midterm Analysis, chapter 4).
- The boards of education in some districts have redefined the role
  of board subcommittees dealing with curriculum and instruction
  and asked them to meet with grade-level and subject-area staff to
  review their progress toward goals (see chapter 2).

As noted, certain factors related to readiness have to be assessed in any
district before implementing changes. Labor relations are an important
factor, and in some cases superintendents may have to weigh what "can"
be done (legally by contract) versus what some members of the district
"want" to be done (based on personal beliefs, philosophy, openness to
change). Whether pushing an unwanted initiative is the best course of action in order to meet the needs of children cannot be answered in this
book or any other. This decision typically falls on the shoulders of the superintendent to determine the risk-reward benefits. In some cases the superintendent may decide that the needs of children are urgent and change
has to occur immediately. In others, the superintendent may determine
that taking several months to lay groundwork will pay off in the long run,
and as a result it is not worth the risk of forcing a new idea.

In the situations described previously, these efforts were considered
to be practical in the first year of implementation. In other districts, perhaps only a couple of ideas could be implemented immediately.

LONG-TERM ACTIONS

One of the foundation principles supporting *Focused Leadership* is
Collaboration, and one of the most important activities to take place in

implementation involves building-level staff members determining what might be done differently that would benefit student learning. These efforts are more systemic in nature, often resulting in practices that become part of district policy and school practices. Where possible, these efforts should be district-wide.

- In one district all of the teachers were asked to participate in a comprehensive curriculum mapping project in the area of social studies. In addition to what they learned immediately about discrepancies in the curriculum, the information they gathered became the basis for a new K–12 curriculum.
- Another district decided that it wanted to conduct a district-wide staff development program focusing on differentiated staffing. Training included administrators as well as teachers. During the next year, the same district focused on a curriculum review.

A number of important benefits result from these comprehensive efforts. The skill and knowledge levels of staff members are increased. In addition, staff members clearly see that the commitment made by the board of education and superintendent is real and not "just another fad." One of the most important benefits comes with the development of a learning culture. Discussions about teaching and learning become a norm rather than an exception.

> In the same district, students who had graduated from the middle school asked their new high school science teacher for a structured overview to use to study from for a test. This teacher, who had refused to participate in staff development programs that taught this concept, came forward and asked for help, joking that he finally had to concede, "If you can't beat 'em, join 'em!"

- As an example, in one district staff meetings at the middle school were dedicated every other Friday morning to sharing. One or two teachers would share teaching strategies they had developed that seemed to work well. People looked forward to these sessions as opportunities to expand their repertoire of instructional strategies.
- Another district, which had made a strong commitment to staff development, established a program in which promising initiatives were identified in relation to the district's mission statement. Each summer the superintendent conducted an administrative retreat,

and a major part of the retreat involved administrators discussing a staff development topic that was to be used in the district during the next school year. Administrators were all required to read a book or series of articles and be prepared to discuss how to implement the staff development, identify outcomes that might be expected, and share ideas on how the new knowledge and skills could be most effectively implemented.

- Taking a "systems approach" was encouraged in all of the districts using *Focused Leadership.* This became a natural outgrowth of first-year implementation once positive student results were reported. Board and staff members want to sustain improvements, and the best way to do this is by institutionalizing practices that appear to make a difference. As a result, reviews and changes took place in the way things had been done historically. Establishing systems in areas such as hiring, tenure, retention, staff development, curriculum development, lesson planning, supervision, and finance have all been adopted in various districts.

THE SMALL PICTURE

Anyone with experience in making changes in a large organization is painfully aware of the time and patience needed to be successful. They are also aware that successes often come one at a time, person by person.

The first year of *Focused Leadership* is challenging since there is so much to do. Getting people to buy into the concepts and begin to look more carefully at what they do and their impact on students is no simple task. Just getting people to focus on what they want and to look at their practices to see if they are in line with desired outcomes is likely to produce positive results.

Although the importance of the first year cannot be overstated, the succeeding years provide the real challenge to board members, administrators, and teachers. The idea is no longer unique, and maintaining the excitement becomes more difficult. Student results in key areas may have jumped significantly, and the challenge may no longer be in seeing large increments of improvement but possibly smaller increments, since there is less space between where students are now functioning and the top. This is not dissimilar to athletes or coaches after they have won major championships. They consistently talk about the excitement that accompanies the first championship, but how hard it is to come back and do it a second time because expectations are now so high and everyone else is using them as a benchmark to improve upon.

Districts that have committed to *Focused Leadership* have used the first year to initiate large-scale initiatives such as staff development and curriculum alignment measures. With these efforts as foundations, direction is established for efforts to take place in subsequent years. One key activity in all of the *Focused Leadership* districts involves the use of summer planning.

- Administrators should conduct summer retreats to review and discuss data related to student outcomes from the year. Data should be compared to goals that were established in relation to other districts of similar makeup (most of the districts tend to use others with comparable socioeconomic makeups, as well as suburban, rural, or city representation), to historical student performance, and any other comparisons that make sense. Exceptions should also be considered. For instance, it is common for results on a particular test, especially one made up annually by a state education department, to be unusually easy or difficult in a given year and therefore not a good tool for discriminating student performance. The following graph and scattergram provide good examples.

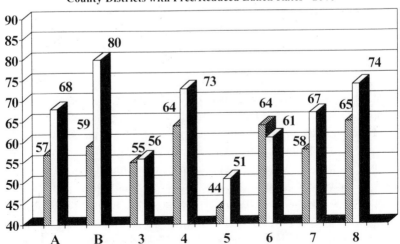

Gr 4 ELA % at Levels 3 or 4: 1999 vs. 2000
County Districts with Free/Reduced Lunch Rates >20%

County School Districts
Math 10 State Test Results

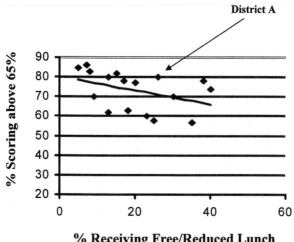

District A

% Scoring above 65%

% Receiving Free/Reduced Lunch

The bar graph compares two *Focused Leadership* districts from the same county. Both districts have a large number of students receiving Free and Reduced Lunch, over 20 percent. Six other districts in the county have more than 20 percent of their students in the Free and Reduced Lunch category, as well. The bar graph shows that District A and District B jumped 19 percent and 36 percent, respectively, in the number of students who scored in levels 3 and 4 of their state's English-Language Arts test after one year of using *Focused Leadership*. In addition, District B was #1 in this group in gains and District A was #2.

Another way of viewing data is through a scattergram showing the relationships of Districts A and B to the fifteen other districts in the county. This compares Districts A and B to the other school districts on the fourth-grade English-Language Arts test. This chart shows the percentage of students scoring at levels 3 and 4 of the test, correlated to the percentage of students receiving free and reduced lunch in each district (a measure of socioeconomic status of the district). Since socioeconomic status of students is the strongest predictor of academic performance, it is important to know if students are scoring better than, poorer than, or about what they would be predicted to score, based on socioeconomic background. Various other methods using statistical analysis can also be extremely useful to administrators and teachers as they try to analyze strengths and weaknesses. Comparisons to neighboring districts, similar districts, and historical trends within one's own district are all useful sources for comparison.

Once administrators have had a chance to review data, decisions need to be made about goals to be recommended to the board. At this point, goals may become narrower than they were previously. For instance, one district had real concerns about the results in its high school math program. The district determined that while concerns became more obvious at the high school due to the amount of test reporting done at that level, the problem was really a K–12 issue. Based on observation, there was agreement that the way math was being taught and the time being committed to it at the elementary level often varied, based on the teacher and his or her comfort with math. As a result, a goal to improve math performance was constructed, with several activities aimed at a comprehensive plan for improvement:

- Mapping of K–12 math curriculum during the next summer;
- Commitment of finances to conduct a review of math programs and purchase a new math series when completed;
- Development of math labs and a means to direct students in need of receiving extra attention;
- Item analysis of tests;
- Hiring of a new math coordinator;
- Staff development;
- Use of a math consultant with a track record of success in working with districts;
- Review of progress by the board's subcommittee on curriculum; and
- Regularly scheduled meetings of math instructors, K–12.

The focus on the math program in this district was a priority as a result of several years of concern. While the concerns had existed, there had never been a plan based on objective data and goals. This kind of information was useful to administrators, who had difficulty convincing many of the math instructors that a real problem did exist. Although math was the major priority area, several other goals continued to receive attention.

Another district conducted a comprehensive review in three curricular areas during its first year: English-language arts, social studies, and math. A panel of teachers, along with the program consultants, was asked to develop a set of observations and recommendations. These provided a plan for activities that needed to occur in the second year. Because of the breadth of the initial effort, a number of suggestions were made:[1]

- Junior high and high school teachers should analyze their curricular maps together on the fall Superintendent's Conference Day and cross-reference them to performance indicators to identify gaps and begin to look for approaches to fill them.
- The director of instruction should develop a newsletter with a unique format to share curriculum-related information with staff members, in addition to regularly scheduling updates through workshops or at faculty meetings.
- Staff members who attend workshops should share what they have learned with colleagues through the new newsletter.
- Revision of the summer curriculum writing proposal application should be instituted, and applicants should be required to reference curriculum maps and audit information as justification for proposed projects.
- Changes should be made in the format of curriculum maps to note the introduction, reinforcement, and mastery of skills.
- Maps should be reviewed by building principals as a means of assuring accountability for meeting core requirements.
- Ideas should be developed with staff on how more time can be focused on curriculum content. One suggestion would be the restructuring of department and grade-level meetings by sharing more operational information via paper or e-mail and/or facilitating vertical department/grade-level meetings. A second suggestion might be the development of interdisciplinary units
- Commitment would be made to try to identify specific resource needs and develop a cycle for purchasing. Make sure purchases are reflected in maps, curriculum, and, ultimately, improved student achievement.
- Need to involve special education and enrichment staff members in a workshop on the current middle-level math curriculum and be sure to invite them to all future workshops when math curriculum changes are explained.
- Will train all elementary teachers and principals in analyzing student performance data and expect them to do this on a regular basis to inform instruction.

- Will train principals at all levels to regularly use student perform-ance data with their staffs to provide guidance for instruction.
- Teacher-made tests should be revised to align with new state stan-dards.

The district that generated these activities had completed its first year in *Focused Leadership* activities, and while the suggestions made here were being implemented in English-language arts, math, and so-cial studies, another group of subjects (physical education, music, art, health, and foreign language, along with special education and enrich-ment staff) was beginning its first year of review

Using the format outlined in the *Program Management Cycle* (see chapter 3), the remaining curricular areas would be reviewed during the third year. Following this, a five-year cycle is planned, with approxi-mately one-fifth of the district's curriculum reviewed once every five years.

As one administrator noted, "The advantage of this approach is that it has required us to put our commitments to paper. That has made us accountable to plan and follow through." Her comment goes to the heart of *Focused Leadership*. With defined goals and responsibilities for all stakeholders, an ongoing process for *Systems Building* is estab-lished. The effort toward improving student achievement is never "over" with the completion of a task or school year. The annual cycle for reviewing different content areas, followed by recommendations and actions, ensures that ongoing attention in the areas most in need will endure. Most important, this process withstands changes in leader-ship, whether the superintendent leaves, board members turn over, or building principals and staff change.

THE BIG PICTURE

Thousands of books and articles have been written on the topic of school culture. For the most part the research on positive cultures is de-scriptive and generally talks about the importance of mission state-ments, difficulties in managing change, and the various other compo-nents that make up school cultures. Writers and researchers have done a magnificent job of describing what cultures are, but less has been written on the topic of how one goes to school on Monday morning and actually constructs a new culture, particularly a "learning culture."

Focused Leadership probably lends itself best to the very simple definition of culture as "the way we do business around here." The districts that have adopted *Focused Learning* as a means of operating their educational program rarely talk about culture. In fact, only when we suggest that they are changing the culture in their districts do we see the eyes of board members and administrators and teachers widen. They don't really think about the fact that they have begun to change the culture of their districts based on any conscious effort. It just happens.

For the first time, boards of education play a meaningful role in establishing expectations for students. To have the tools to do this, they must know something about data and performance. They also are asked to monitor and follow up with supportive action. Administrators and teachers are required to talk about student results, using many of the recommendations described in the previous pages. Everyday practices, such as evaluation and budgeting, are rooted in student goals when being exercised. Periodic assessments such as midterm and final exams are regularly disaggregated in order to analyze performance. Staff development days are no longer based on what the majority of respondents requested on a checklist but rather are determined by the skills needed by staff members to better serve students' needs. The role of administrators, as Superintendent Larry Rowe of Johnson City puts it, is clear: *If the building principal is not the most knowledgeable person in the building about improving kids' performance, he can't make it here.*

SUMMARY

Several years ago I remember asking a friend who was an assistant superintendent for curriculum if his district had jumped onto the bandwagon that was so popular, revolving around the latest supervision model. He said no, his district had adopted a commitment to teaching reading in the content areas some ten years earlier and was continuing to provide support for that initiative. I was surprised. Teaching reading in the content areas had come and gone and, after all, "everybody" was doing this new supervision model. My friend said that he understood that, but his staff members had a commitment and desire to continue down the track they were on, and furthermore, when they looked at the performance of their children, the students were doing as well or better than those in comparison districts. He said their plan was to wait a couple of years, let his neighbors iron out the bugs, and then they would look at what pieces of the supervision model they might want to adopt.

The tendency to jump from one bandwagon to the next is something that people on the outside, as well as people within education, criticize us for. Yet we continue this practice with such regularity that it has become a norm. We can find any number of critics of the standards movement who decry this as yet the latest in a series of fads, pointing to the use of public report cards as nothing more than a means for making richer districts look better and poorer districts look worst. The critics have a valid point. Those who wish to use these results as barometers for the success or failure of particular schools have enough information available to them to have a field day. While pockets of urban and rural poor schools have had very good success with improving student achievement, there is no doubt that the multiple factors related to socioeconomic status have much more to do with the overall performance of a school than any others do, and this remains an extremely challenging problem for all of society. However, using report cards for this purpose alone is shameful.

Good data, whether it is part of a public report card or not, is one of the most valuable assets that school leaders have available to them. What is important is to utilize valid data as a tool to support improvement. Good information may tell us that we are reteaching a skill in fourth grade that students had already learned in third grade. Consequently, the fourth-grade teacher can spend those three days dedicated to that skill on another topic. Good information may tell us that the physics teacher is asking students to do math calculations in the fall, although the skills needed to do them are not being taught by the math teacher until the winter semester. Good information may also tell us that five of the twenty-four students in a particular first-grade class need further help in decoding words before they will be able to go on and that an alternative must be developed or they are destined to become frustrated and lost.

Along with having good information, it is important that classroom teachers know that success or failure is not totally on their shoulders. Done well, teaching is the most challenging and difficult job in the world. It is also the most rewarding. Board members I have known have typically felt that what they did at the board table had little to do with the performance of students in the schools. They do not need to feel this way, and *Focused Leadership* can help bridge this gap. There is a role for everyone. There are also certain boundaries that are not to be crossed—board members should continue to look at the big picture, set strategic goals, monitor results, and provide a conduit to the community. Administrators should continue to supervise the programs that are in place in the schools, and teachers will have the very important role of delivering education to students on a day-to-day basis.

What is different is that the main purpose of the school—educating students—is truly seen as a shared responsibility. This means trusting that teachers, board members, and administrators all want the same thing for children. It means that when children succeed, everyone succeeds. It also means that when performance is below par, all parties must be willing to stand back, take a deep breath, and determine what "we" need to do in order to improve. This should be the essence of schools. Forget the politics, remember the children.

NOTE

1. Recommendations developed by Judy Morgan, director of Instructional Services and staff from the East Syracuse-Minoa (New York) Central School District.

About the Author

Richard T. Castallo, Ed.D. is Professor of Education at SUNY Cortland as well as coordinator of their Educational Administration Program. He has spoken at hundreds of Board of Education and Administrator retreats.